DEDICATION

This book is dedicated
to you, and all aspiring artists!

Happy Drawing!

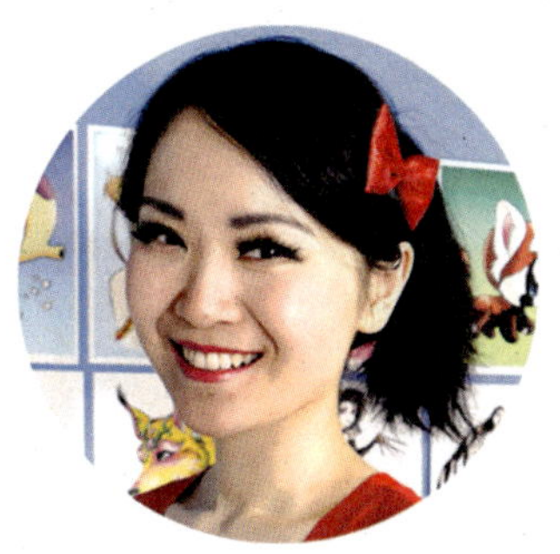

COPYRIGHT

Paperback ISBN: 978-1-990391-47-7
eBook ISBN: 978-1-989939-29-1
First Published October 2021
Book design, cover design, and illustrations by Mei Yu.

For business inquiries, please contact Mei Yu.

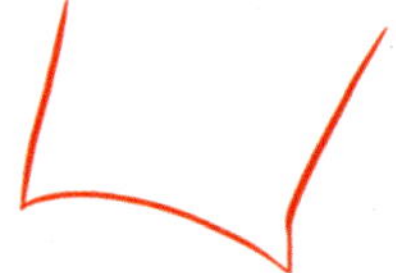

1.
Let's draw the foot with simple shapes first.

Start with the ankle.

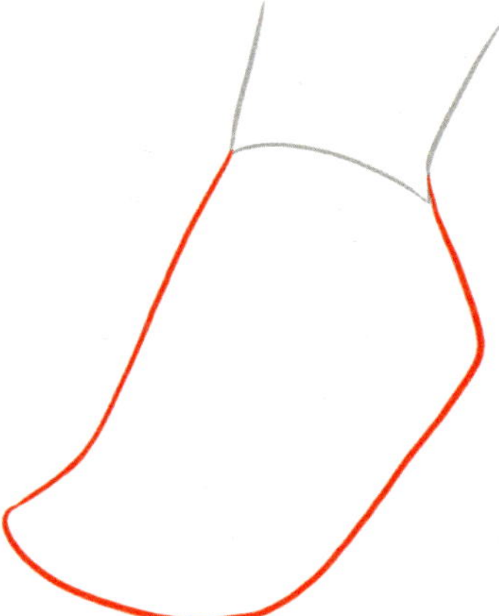

2.
Summarize the foot as a round rectangle.

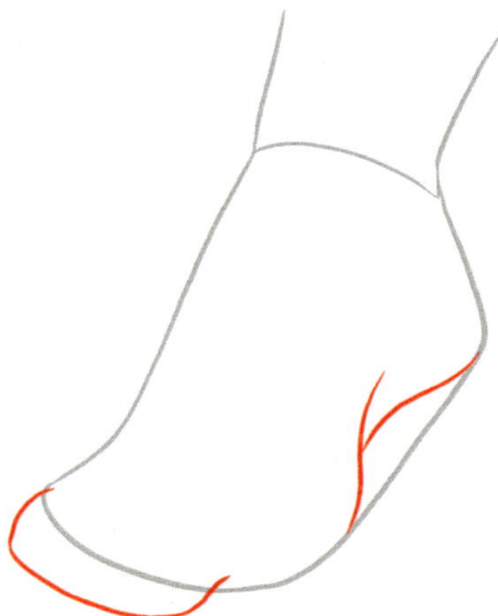

3.
Draw the arch of the foot with curves. Then, add the toe area.

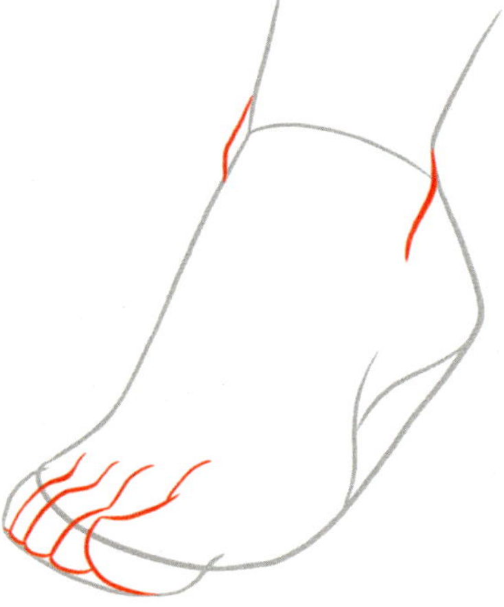

4.
Use curved lines to draw the toes. Make the big toe tilt up for a natural pose.

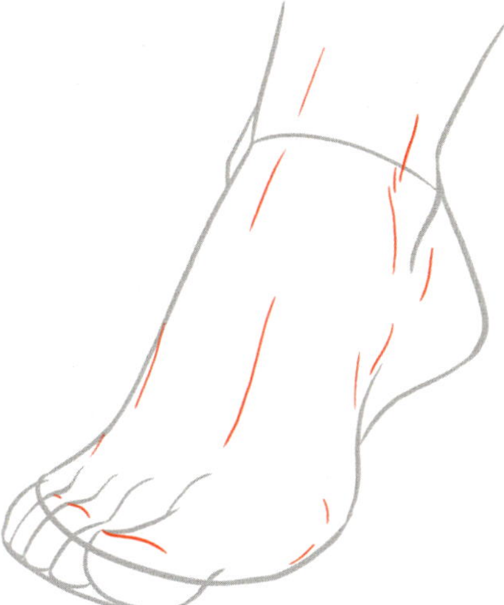

5.
Add finishing touches
for more realism!

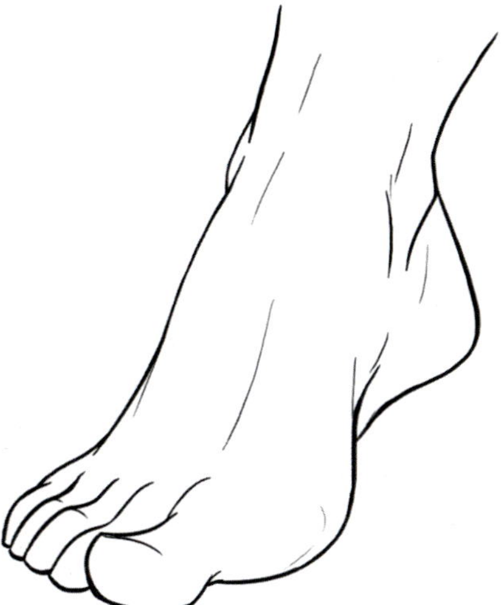

6.
Great job! Now finalize
your lovely foot.

This is a versatile pose for characters in many situations. He could be standing firm and confidently, he could be sitting and relaxing on the beach, or he could be stepping into a pool.

Learn to draw the other foot poses in this book so you can enhance your own characters!

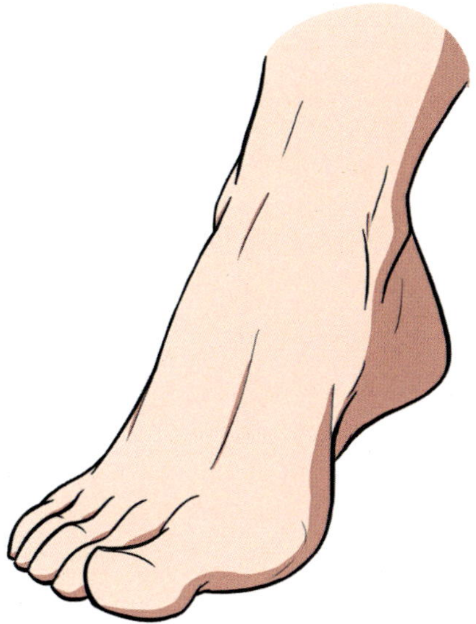

Foot Lying on the Side

BY MEI YU

1.
Begin with the ankle.

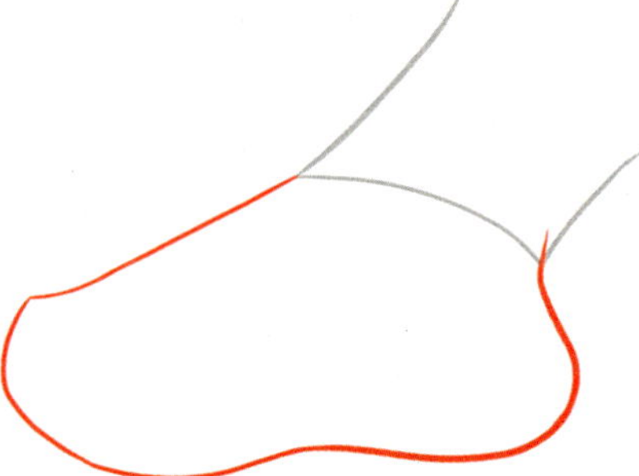

2.
Add a large, soft wedge shape for the main part of the foot.

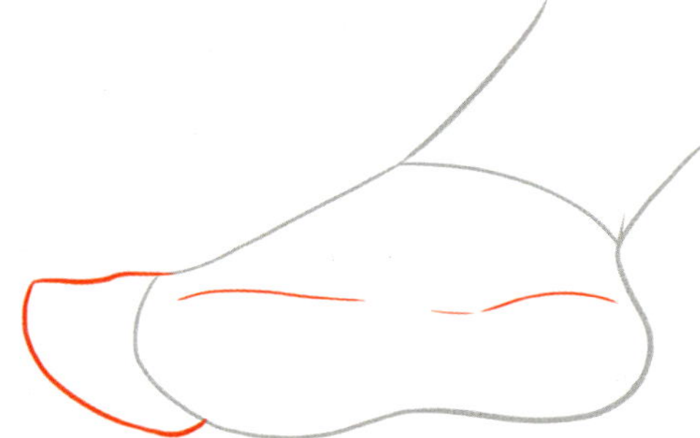

3.
Add the toe area. Show the edge of the foot with some curved lines going across.

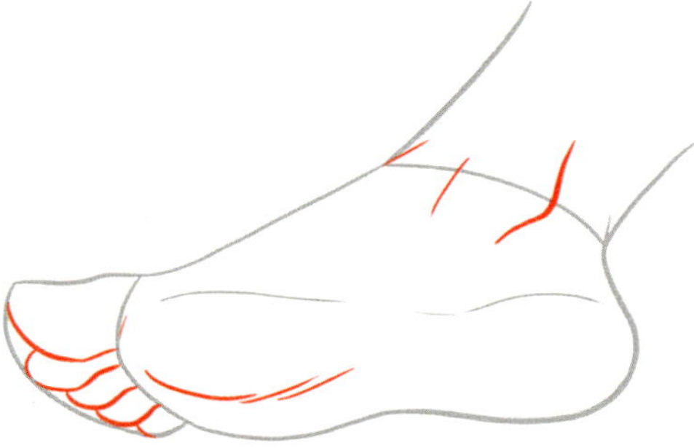

4.
Divide the toes, then add finishing details for the ankle bone and the bottom.

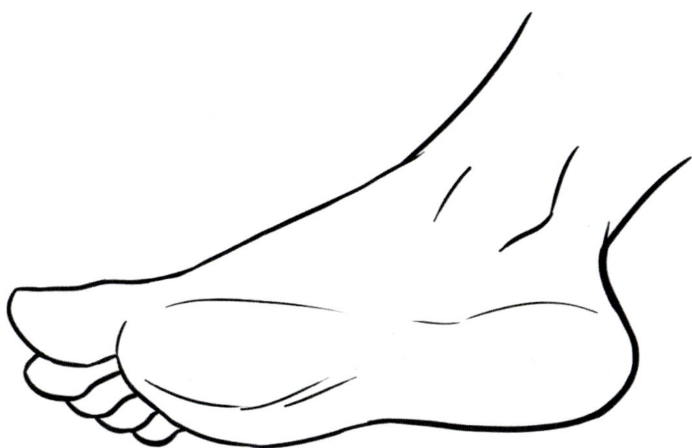

5.
Use a dark pen or marker to go over the final lines.

This is a nice pose for a character who is sleeping or lying on his side.

He could also be about to step on something, or kicking something light.

Try drawing more poses with the female edition of this book to enhance your female characters!

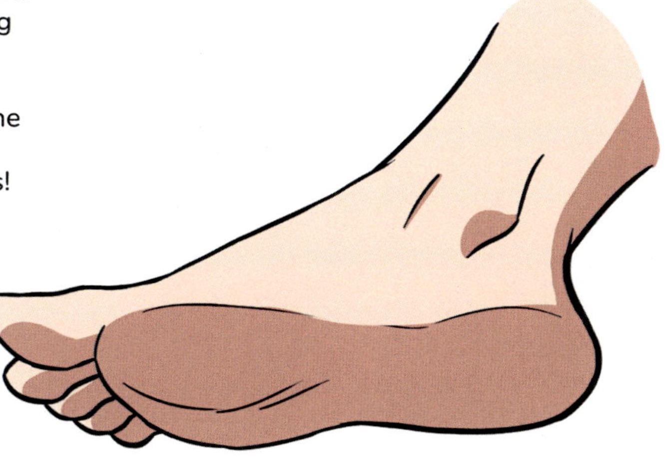

BY MEI YU

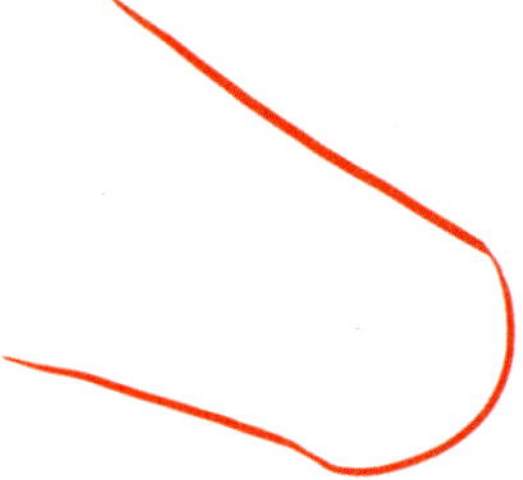

1.
Draw the lower leg tapering into the ankle. If you want your character to look strong, try not to make the ankle too slim.

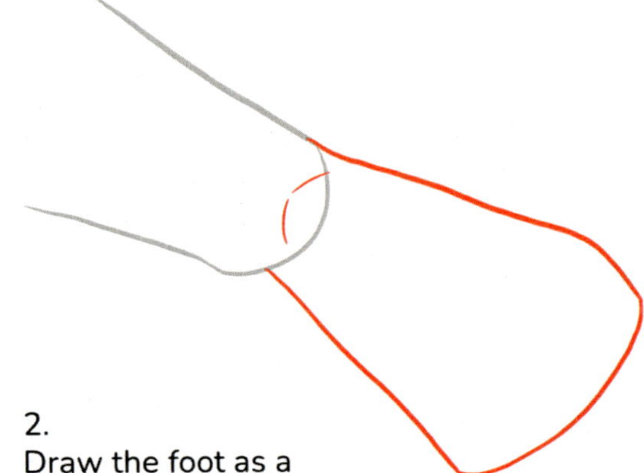

2.
Draw the foot as a wedge shape with the ankle area smaller than the toe area.

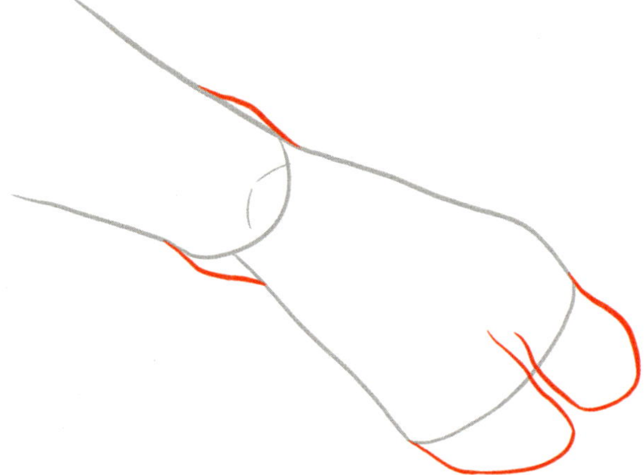

3.
Draw the big toe with a round end, then a general shape for the other toes for now.

Add the ankle bones on both sides of the joint.

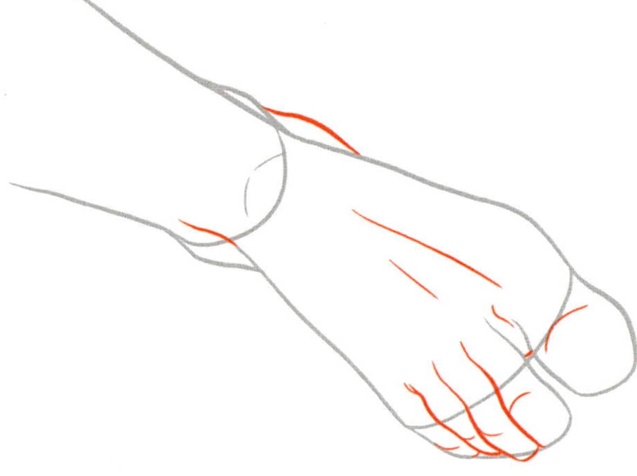

4.
Draw lines going to the toes to make the structure of the foot look strong. Add the rest of the toes, and a little bit of the heel showing on one side in the back.

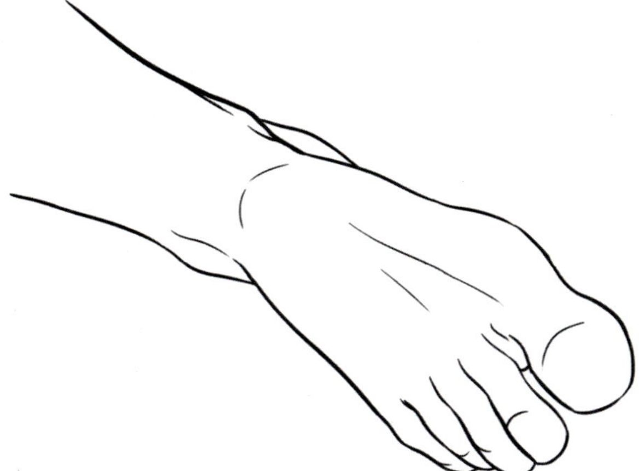

5.
Use your choice of a dark pen, outliner, or marker to go over the final lines.

Try making the little details thin so they don't make the drawing look too heavy.

This is a cool pose for a character who might be kicking something on the side of his foot. Tilt the pose down, and it's good for a standing position.

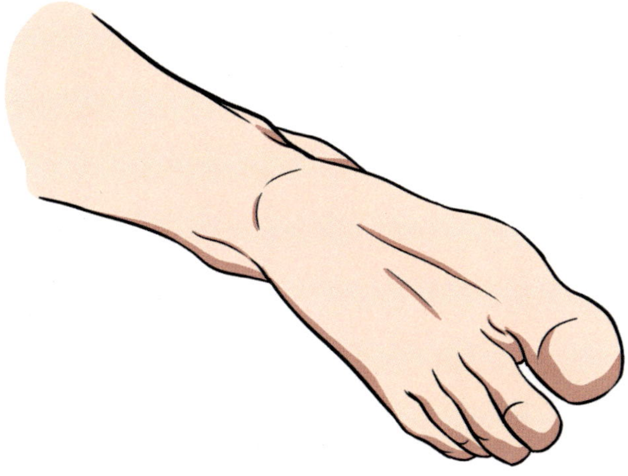

BY MEI YU

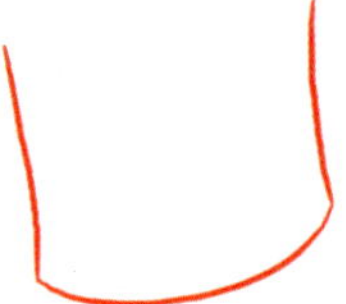

1.
Draw a thick ankle.

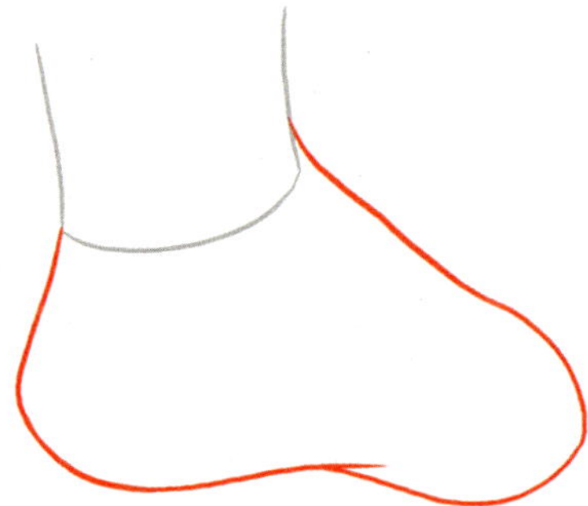

2.
Draw the foot as a round, soft triangle. Make the bottom of the foot curved up for the arch.

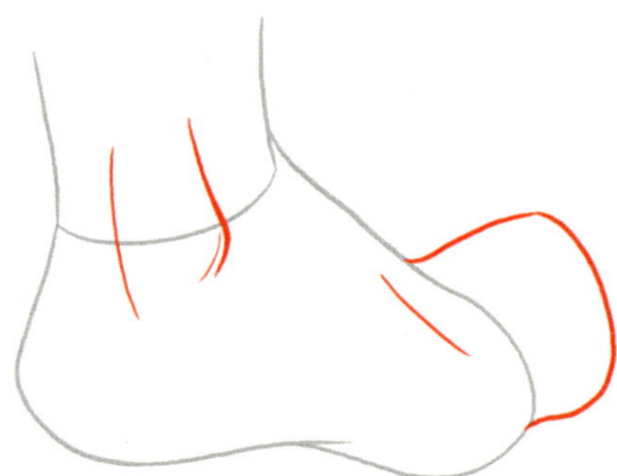

3.
Add the toe area, then draw some lines to show the structure of the foot.

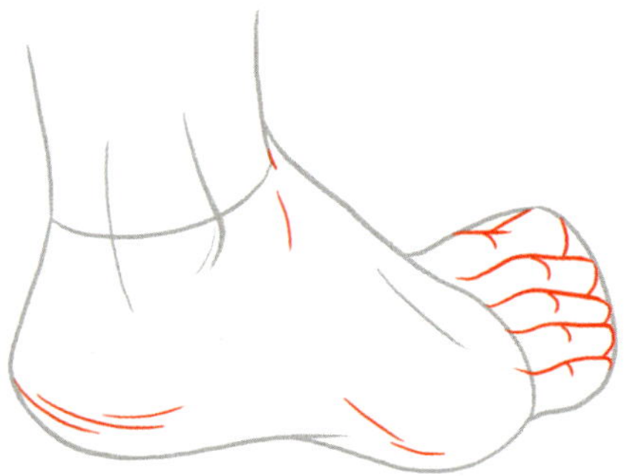

4.
Divide the toe area into the toes with curved lines. Add small curves inside for the joints.

Back 3/4 View

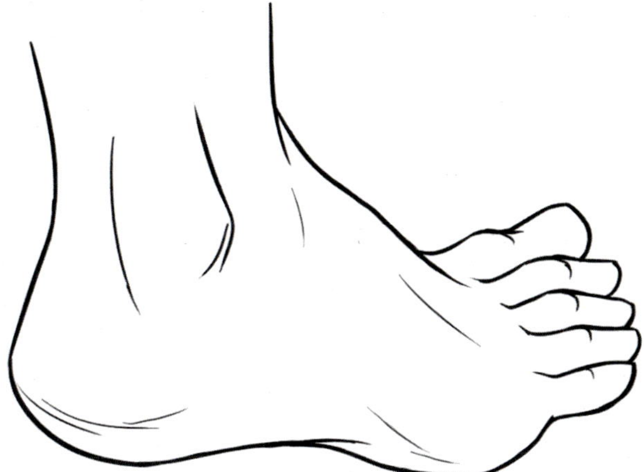

5.
Erase extra lines and finalize your drawing with a dark pen. Try to keep small lines thin, so they won't appear too heavy.

This is a nice view that is between a side view and a back view.

Using front or back 3/4 poses like this can help give your character more of an organic, casual feel, rather than just drawing their feet in strict profile views.

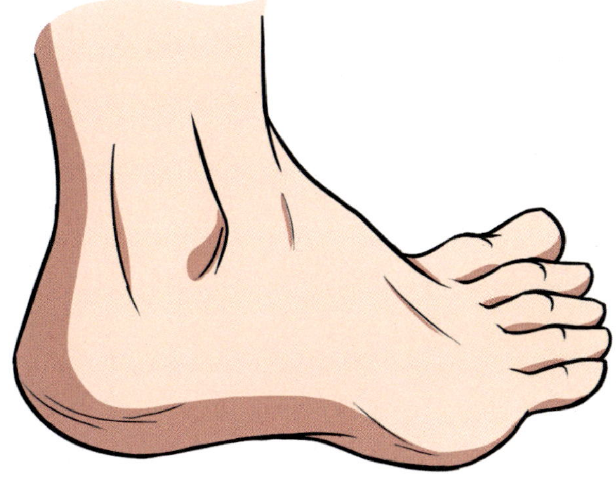

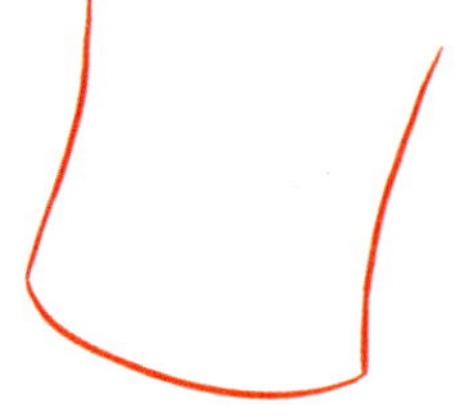

1.
Begin with the ankle.

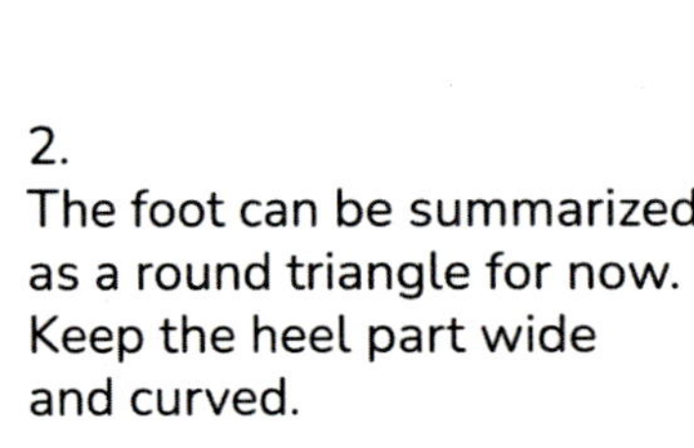

2.
The foot can be summarized as a round triangle for now. Keep the heel part wide and curved.

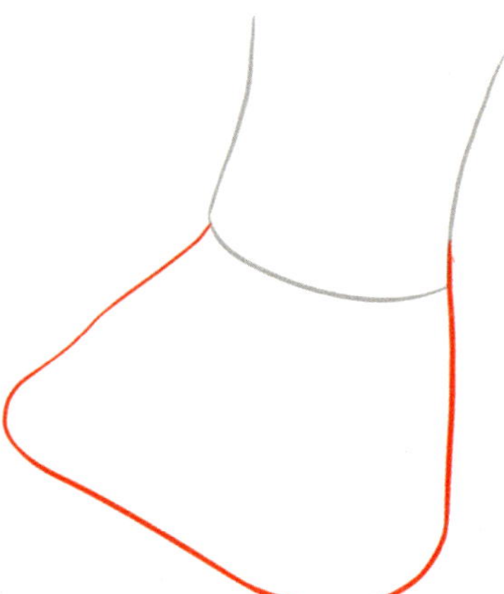

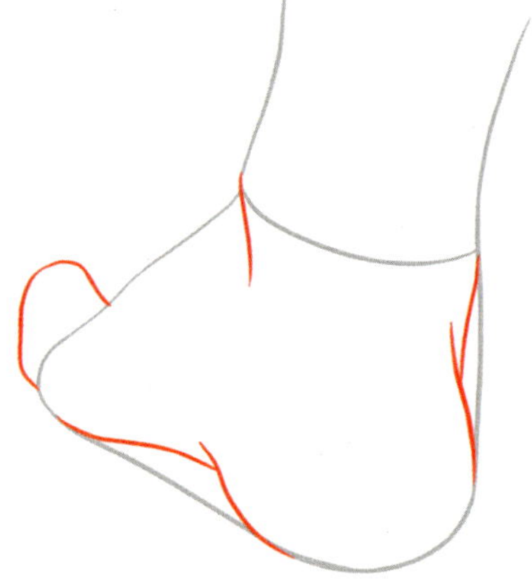

3.
Draw curves in the bottom of the foot to show the arch. Add lines to the heel, then add the big toe.

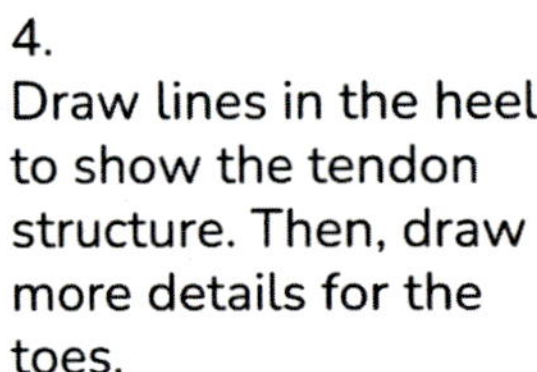

4.
Draw lines in the heel to show the tendon structure. Then, draw more details for the toes.

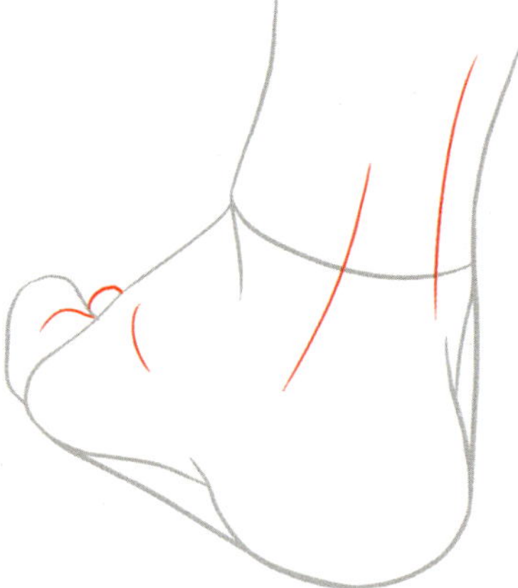

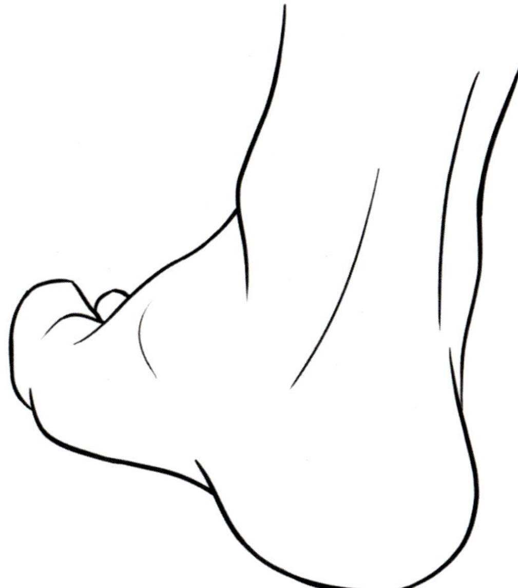

5.
Finalize your drawing with a dark pen or marker.

A great angle for a character's foot!

This can be good for a situation where you want to emphasize the foot, either for suspense, mystery, or for giving your drawing a sense of perspective.

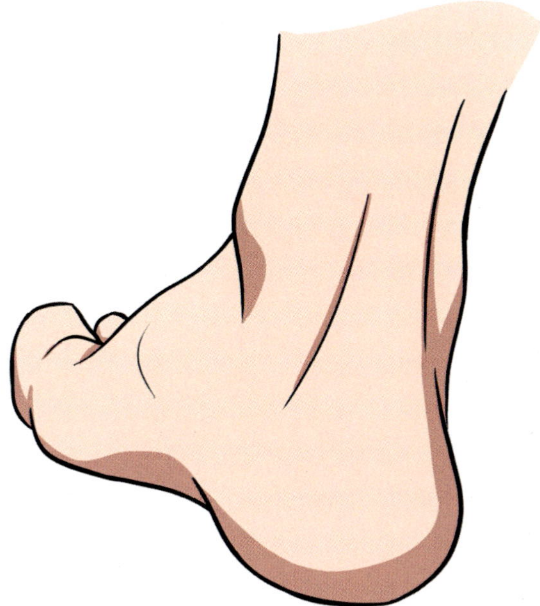

Foot Stepping Firmly

BY MEI YU

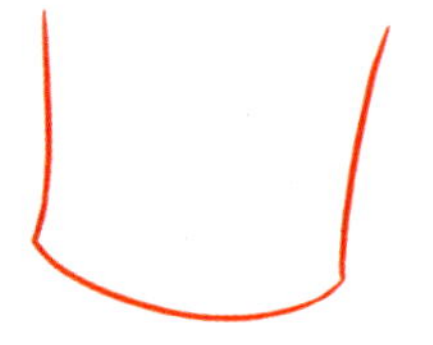

1.
Let's start with the ankle like an open tube.

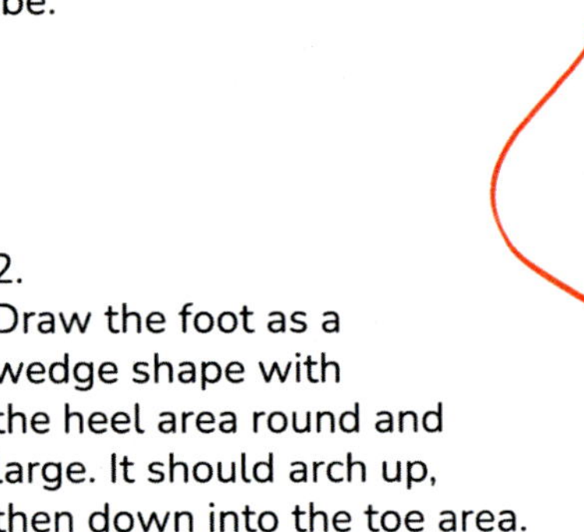

2.
Draw the foot as a wedge shape with the heel area round and large. It should arch up, then down into the toe area.

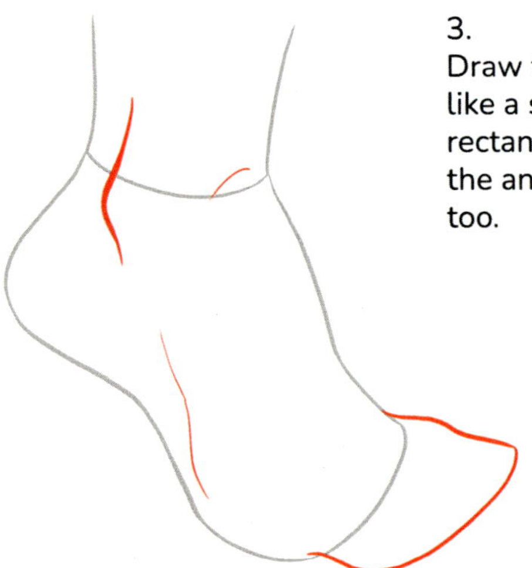

3.
Draw the toe area like a slanted, wide rectangle. Draw the ankle bone, too.

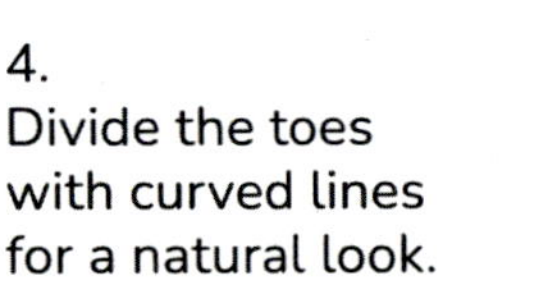

4.
Divide the toes with curved lines for a natural look.

To make the foot look strong and firm, add small details and lines.

Foot Stepping Firmly

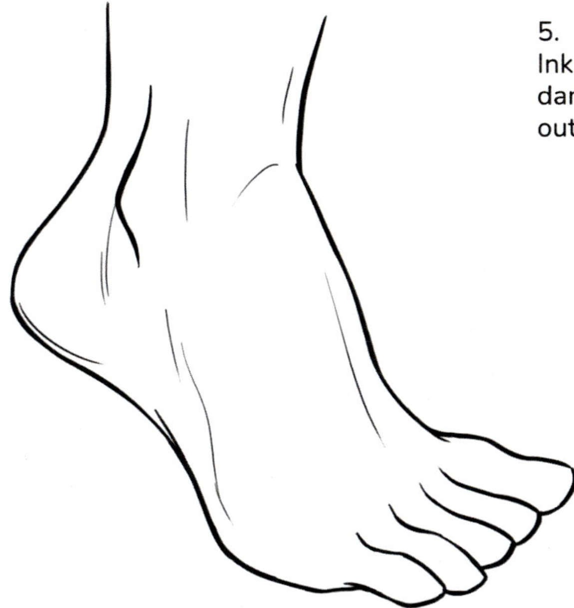

5.
Ink your drawing with a dark marker, thin pen, or outliner.

This is a great pose for a character who is steadfast in his resolve!

He could be stepping firmly and confidently, or pushing against something.

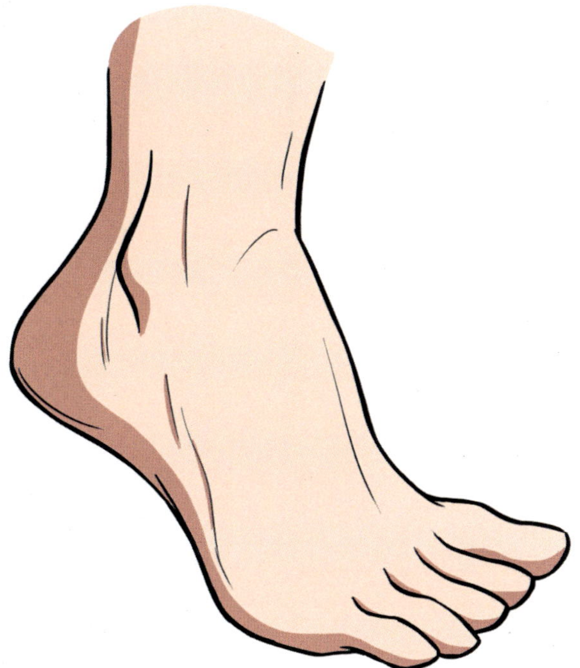

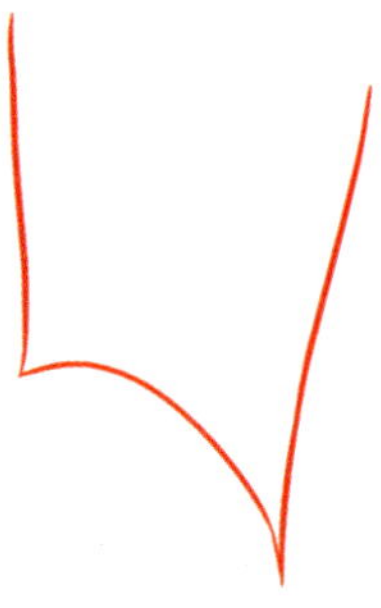

1.
Begin with the ankle.

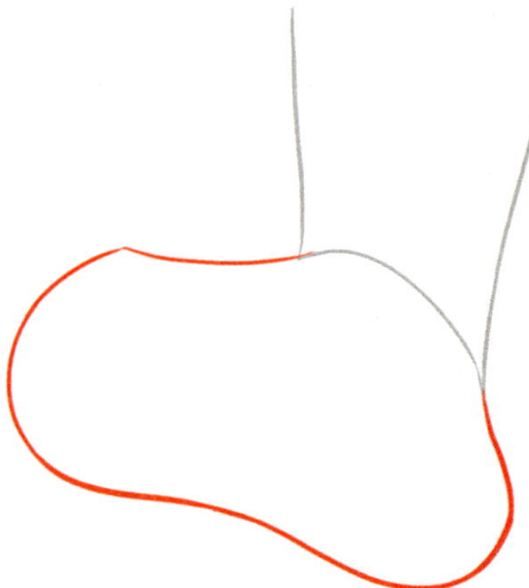

2.
Draw the foot as a large, round bean shape. Try to make the heel part thick and curved.

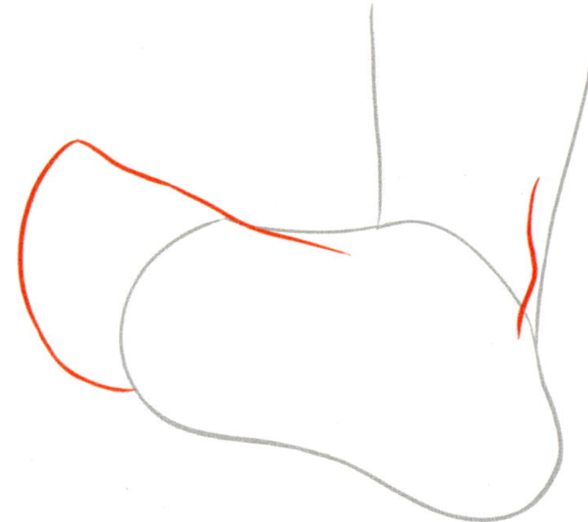

3.
Draw a large, pointy toe area. The top tip will be for the big toe.

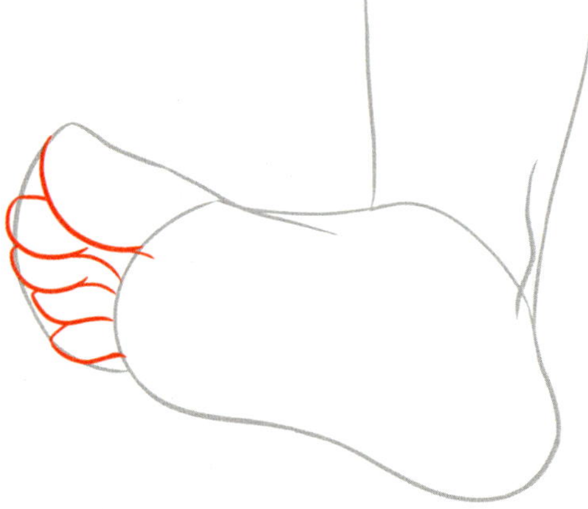

4.
Divide the toe area into the toes with curved lines. The big toe should be the largest.

Strong Kick

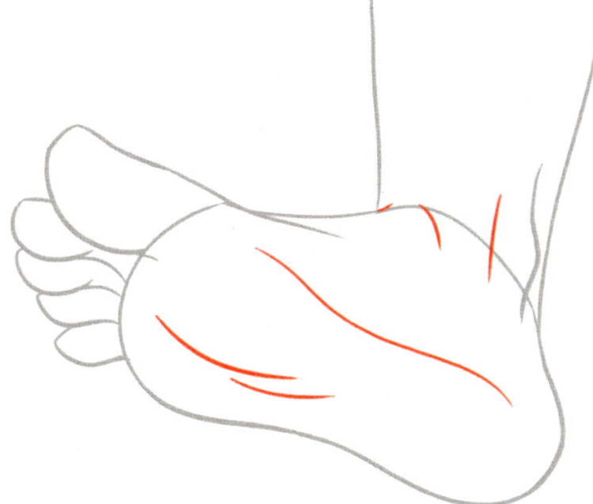

5.
Add details like the curves and edges of the foot for more realism.

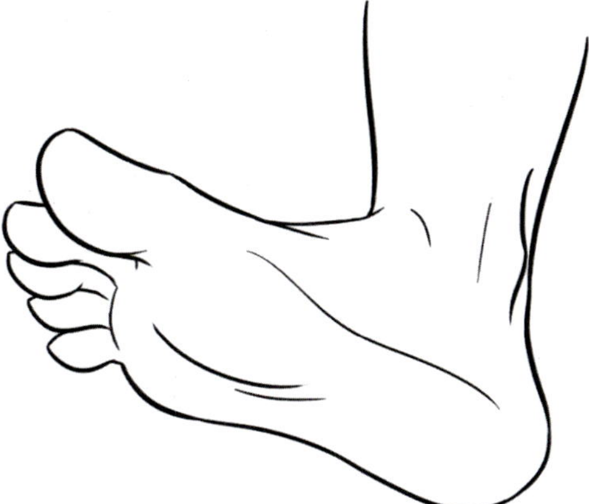

6.
Erase extra lines, then finalize your drawing with a dark pen or marker.

This pose is great for characters who are kicking things, or about to step down on something bad.

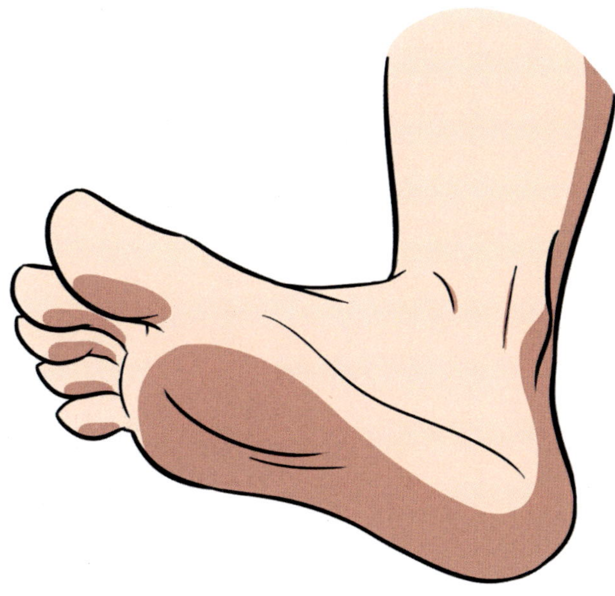

Foot Lifted (Back View)

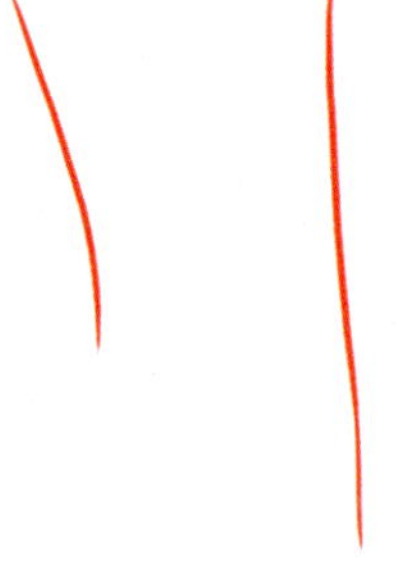

1.
Draw the lower leg with the ankle tapered in a bit.

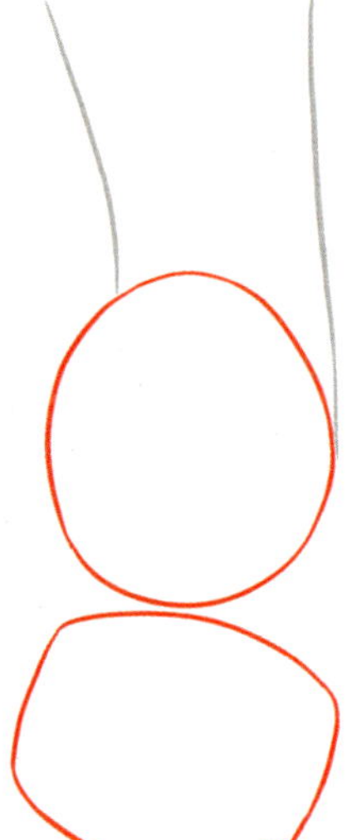

2.
Draw the bottom part of the foot facing the viewer. Begin with two large shapes for now.

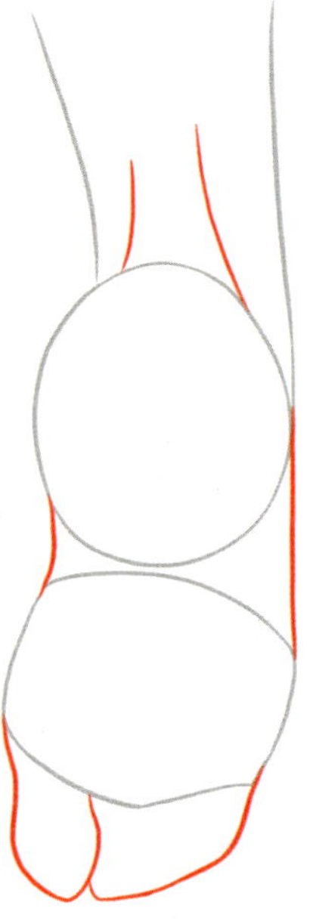

3.
Draw sides to connect the two shapes. Then, add the toe area.

For the heel tendon, add two lines tilted towards each other going from the heel into the ankle.

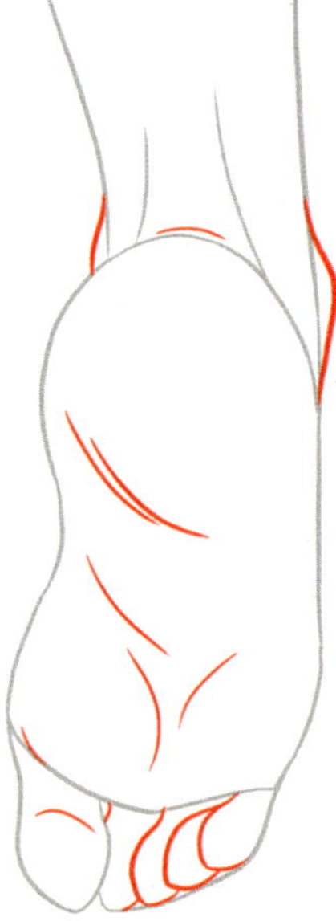

4.
Draw toes with curved lines, then add details like soft folds and the ankle bones.

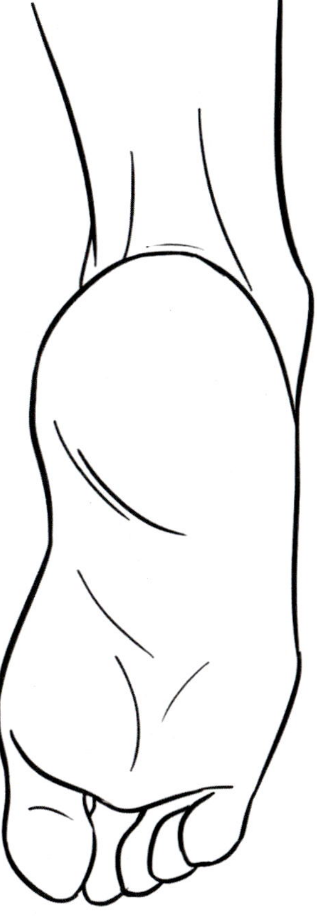

5.
Finalize your drawing!

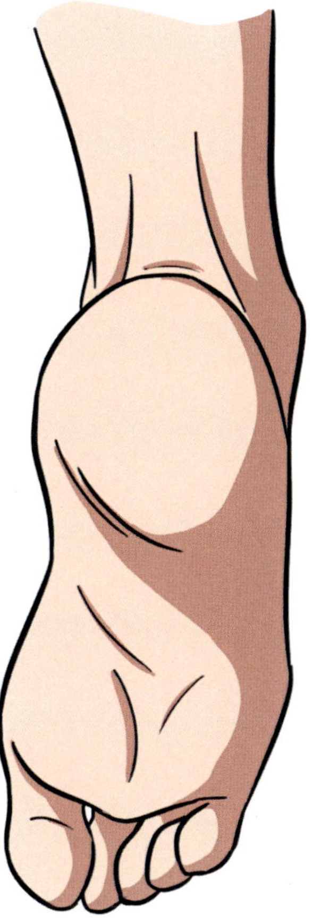

This character could be leaping in the air, sitting on the edge of something, or lifting his foot up.

Front View Foot

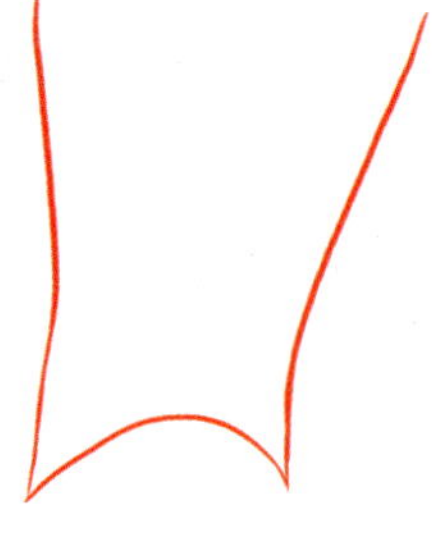

1.
Draw the lower leg tapering into the ankle.

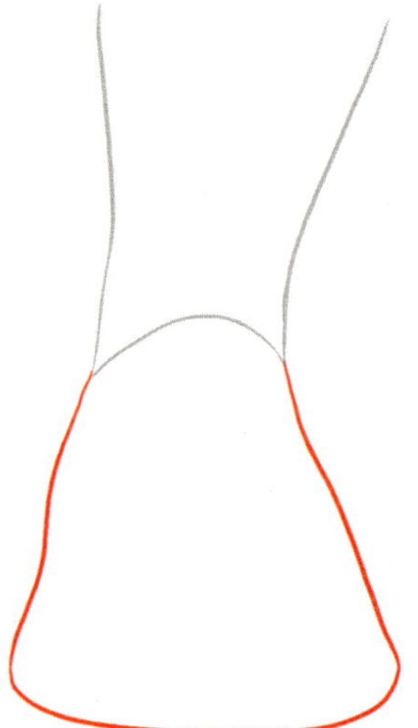

2.
Make the foot like a wide, soft triangle.

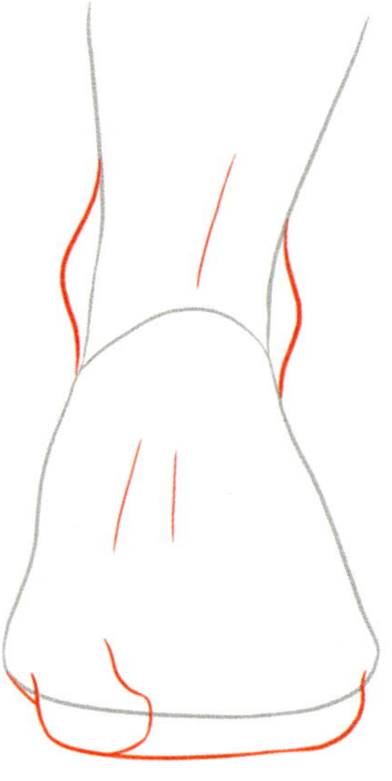

3.
Add a wide toe area with a curved big toe.

For the ankle bones, make them like soft bumps on either side.

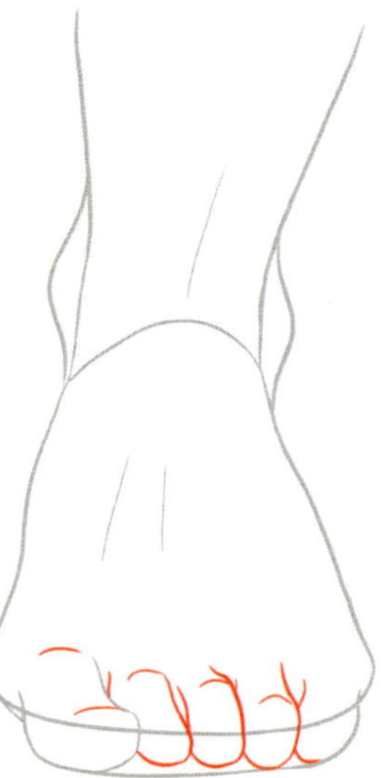

4.
Draw the smaller toes with short, curved lines.

Draw small curves inside the toes to show the bend of the joints.

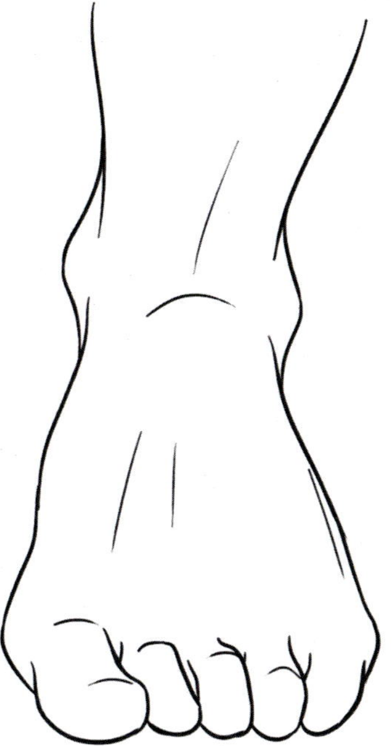

5.
Go over the final drawing with a dark pen or marker.

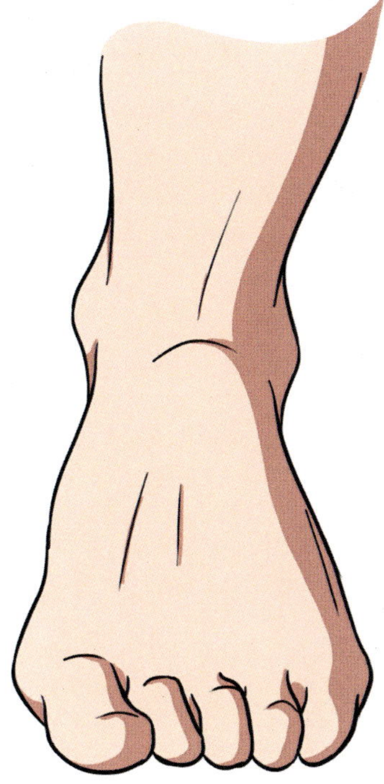

This character could be crouching, squatting, or running. The weight of the character is making the foot squished and wider.

Ouch!

BY MEI YU

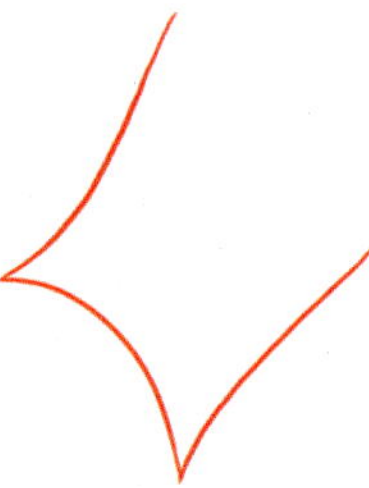

1.
Start with the ankle tapering in from the lower leg.

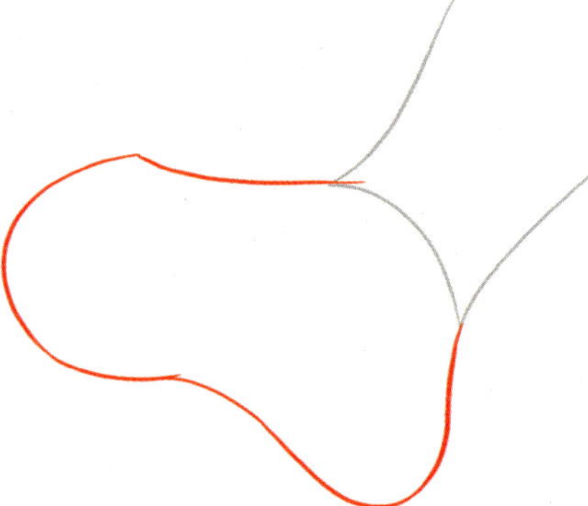

2.
Draw the foot as a wedge shape with a round heel.

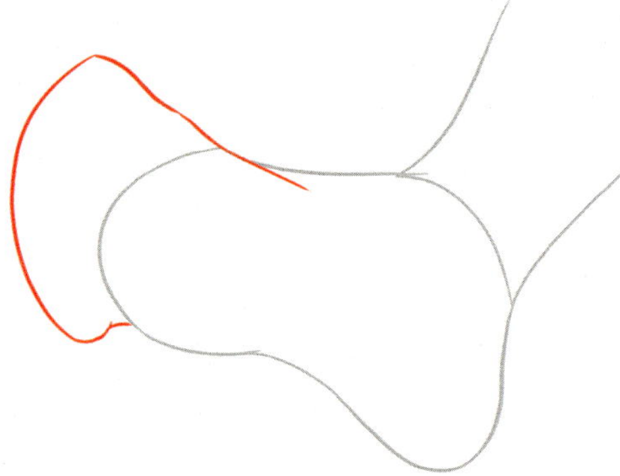

3.
Draw the toe area wide - the toes will fan out in this pose.

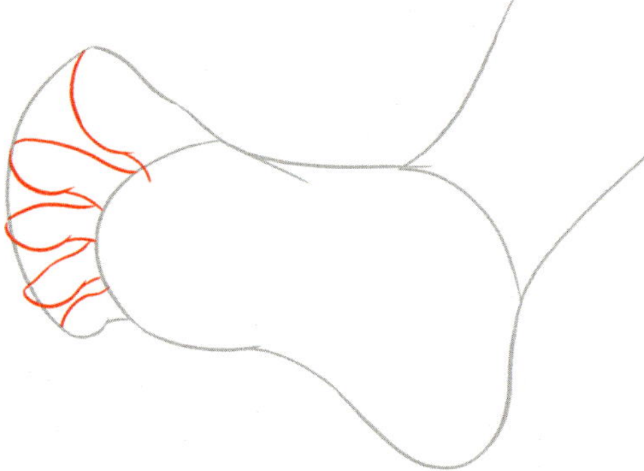

4.
Divide the toes and make them far apart from each other. This is great to show a character in surprise or pain.

Ouch!

5.
Draw finishing touches to make the drawing more realistic. Add small edges to show the form and structure of the foot.

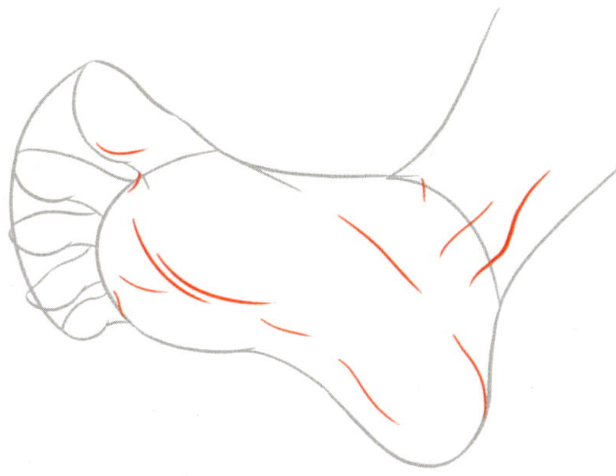

6.
Erase extra lines, then finalize your drawing.

This character could have stepped on something sharp, surprising, or gross. He could also be hurting from another part of his body.

Surprise could also cause this pose - this character could be getting tackled, or jumped by his little sister wanting a piggyback ride... *again*.

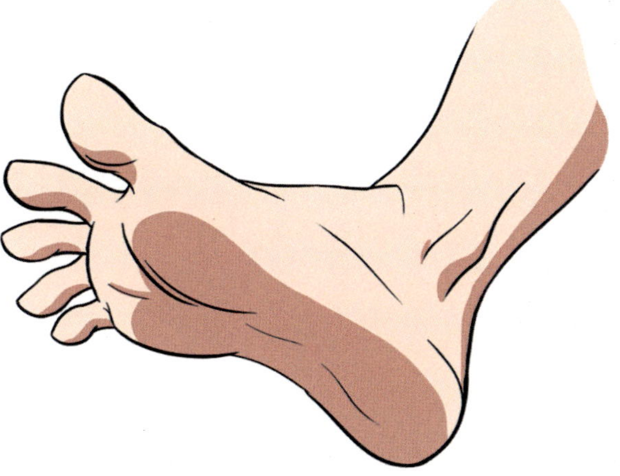

Foot Pointed Down

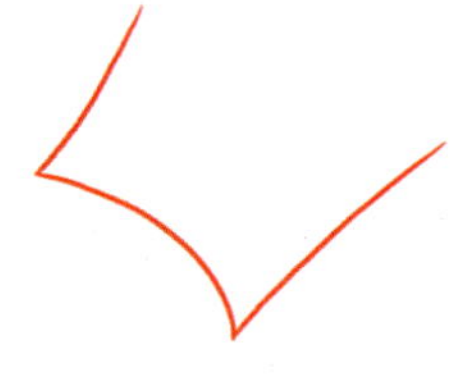

1.
Start with
the ankle.

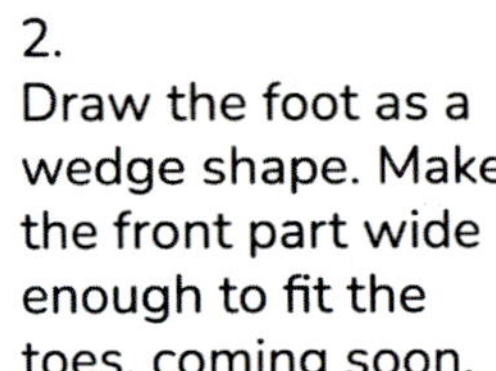

2.
Draw the foot as a
wedge shape. Make
the front part wide
enough to fit the
toes, coming soon.

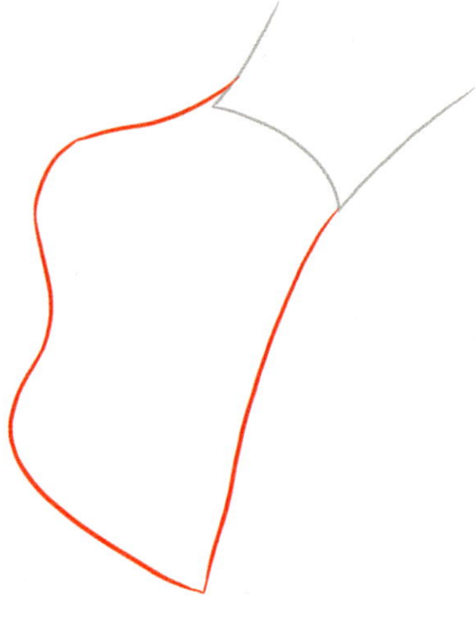

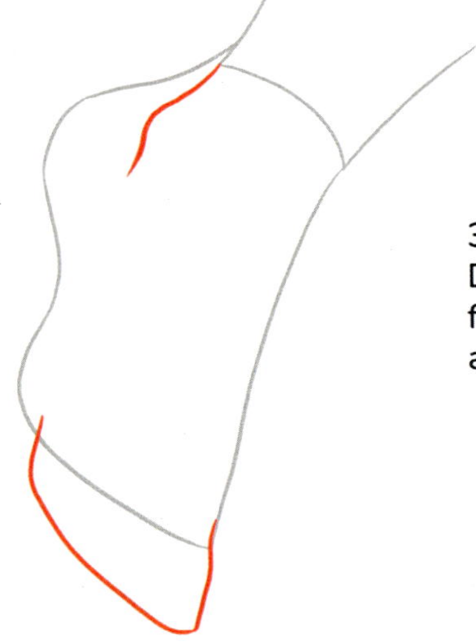

3.
Draw another shape
for the toes. Add the
ankle bone.

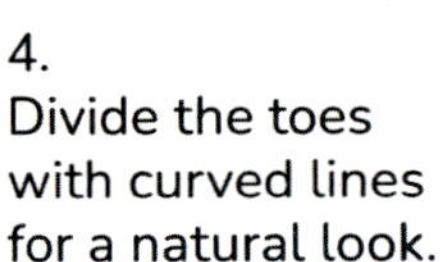

4.
Divide the toes
with curved lines
for a natural look.

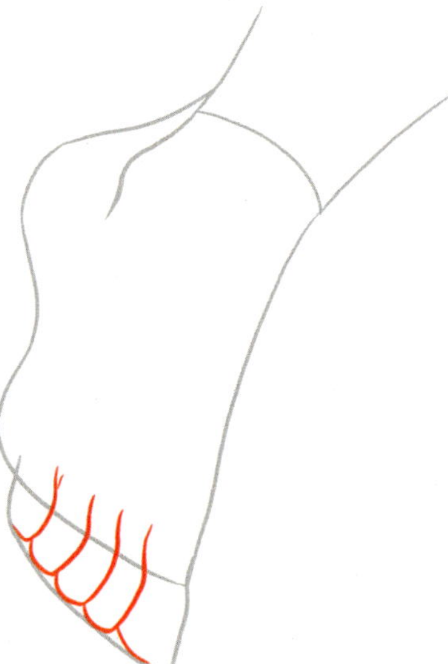

Foot Pointed Down

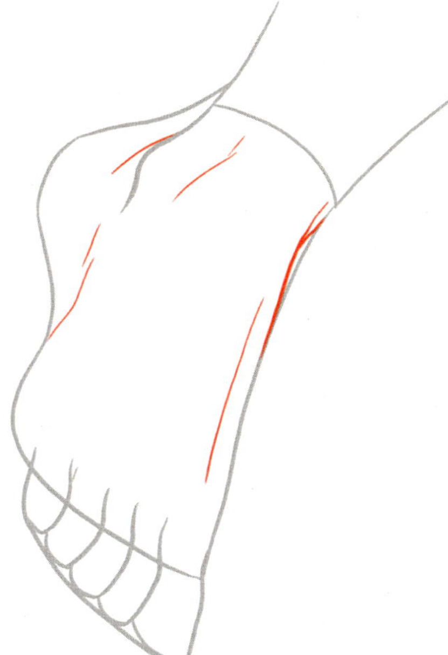

5.
Draw finishing details for more realism.

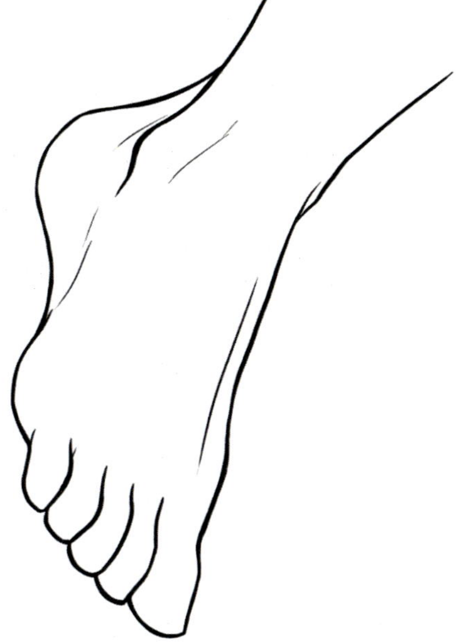

6.
Finalize your drawing!

This pose can be good for when a character is swinging his foot down, or about to kick something.

Angle it forward, and he can have his foot firmly planted on the floor. Experiment to suit your characters!

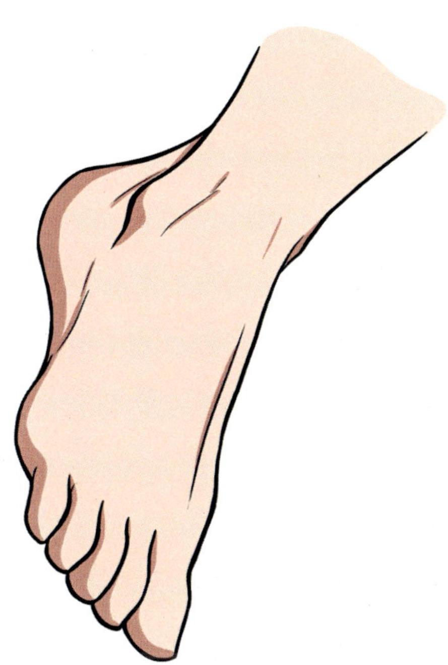

About to Stomp!

BY MEI YU

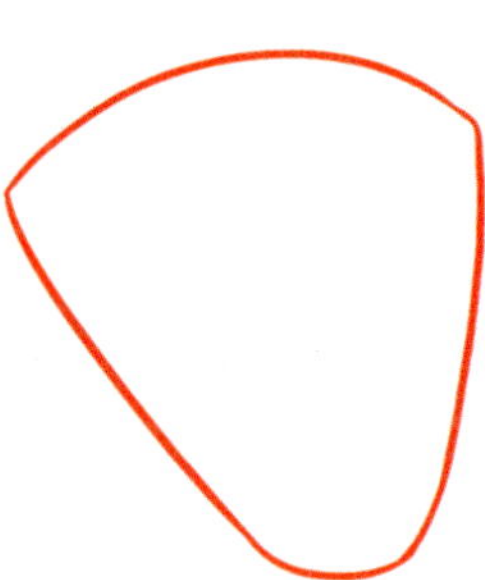

1.
Begin with a round triangle.

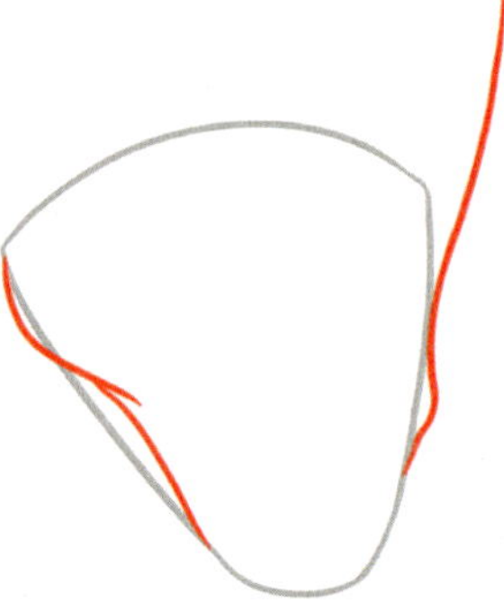

2.
Add curves for the bottom arch of the foot, and the side.

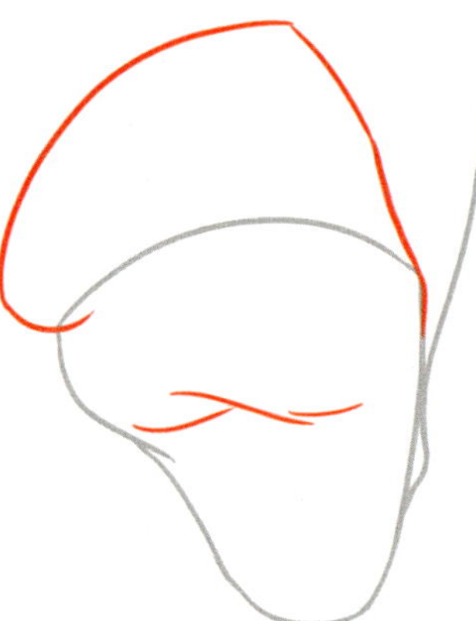

3.
Make the toe area large to emphasize the perspective. This foot can be coming down very close to the viewer!

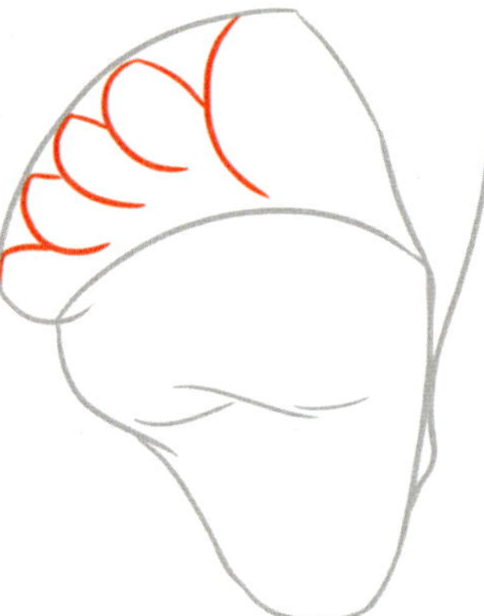

4.
Divide the toe area into curved toes. Make the big toe wider and taller than the others.

About to Stomp!

5.
Draw finishing details and lines for the rest of the toes.

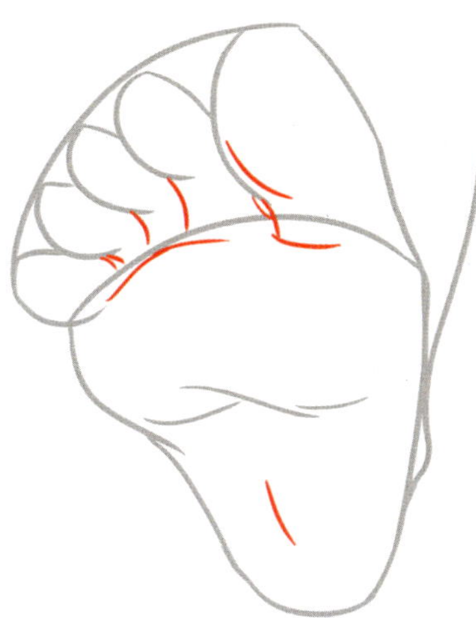

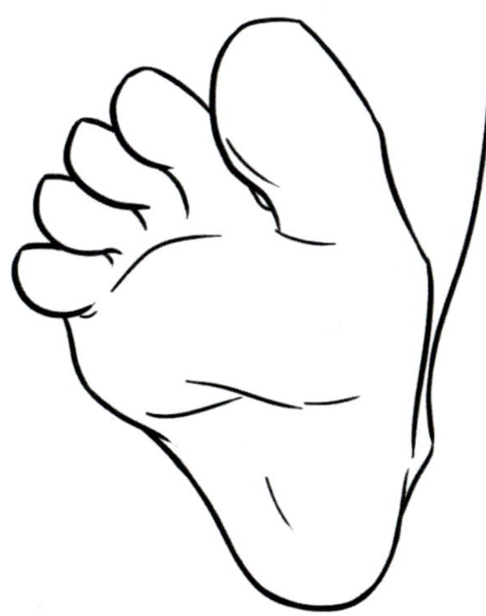

6.
Erase extra lines before inking your drawing with your choice of a dark pen, marker, or outliner.

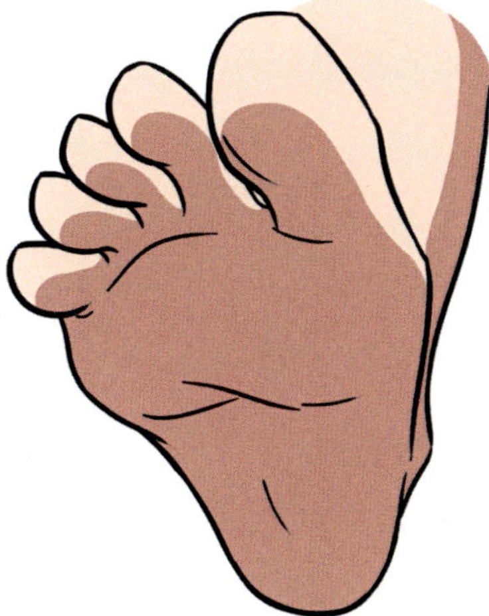

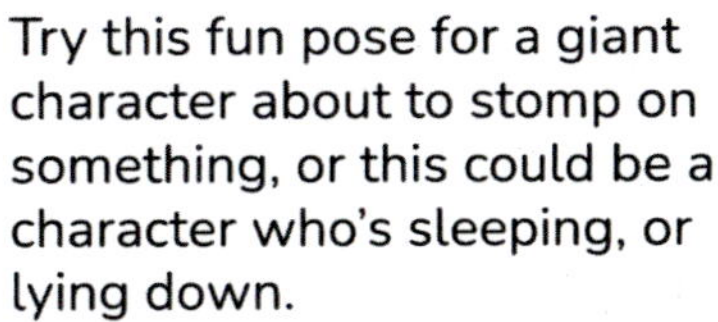

Try this fun pose for a giant character about to stomp on something, or this could be a character who's sleeping, or lying down.

Toes Pointing in the Air

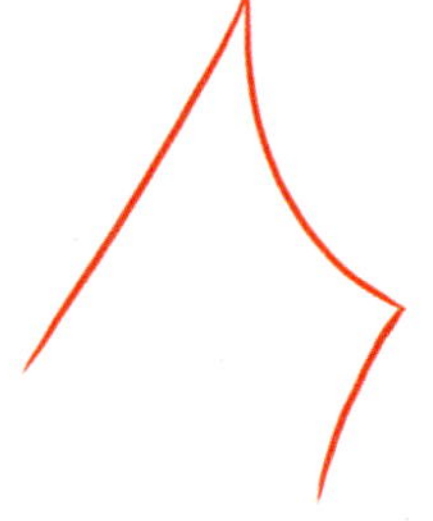

1.
Draw the ankle
tilted up.

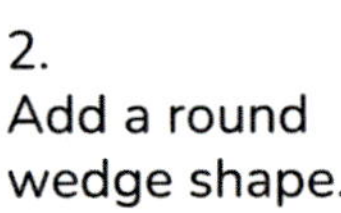

2.
Add a round
wedge shape.

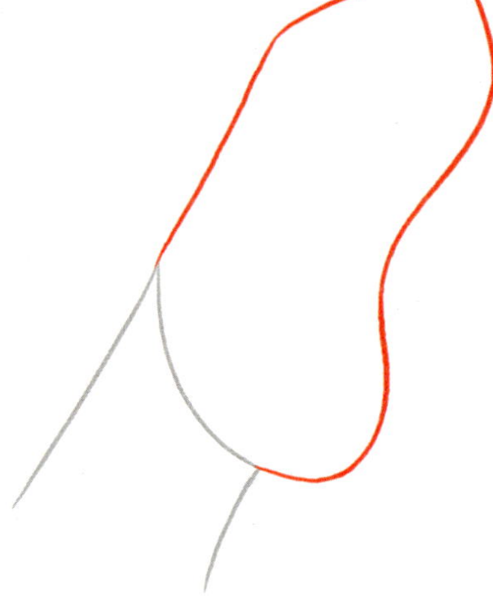

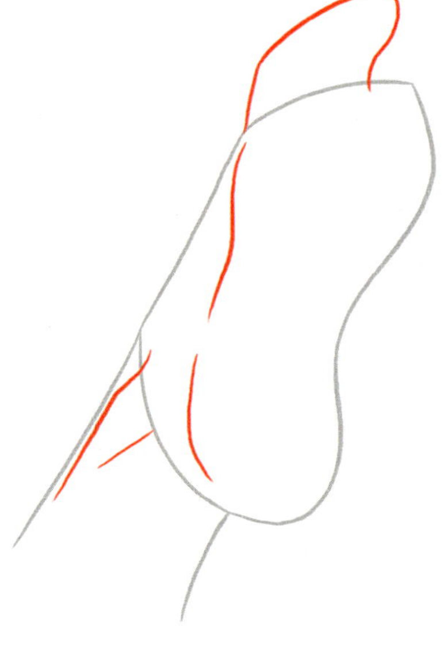

3.
Start the toe shape,
and some lines for
the foot's edges
and bone structure.

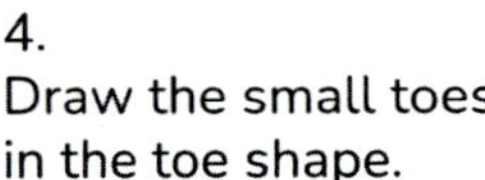

4.
Draw the small toes
in the toe shape.

Then, draw a big
toe beside them.

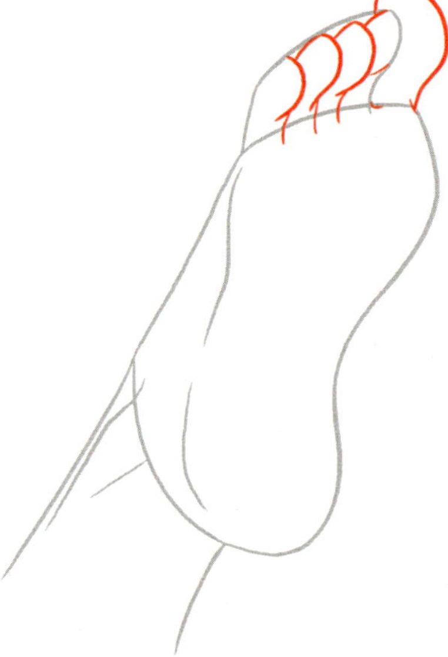

5.
Make the foot look sturdy and realistic with small texture and crease lines.

Add lines around major bent areas, like at the back of the heel.

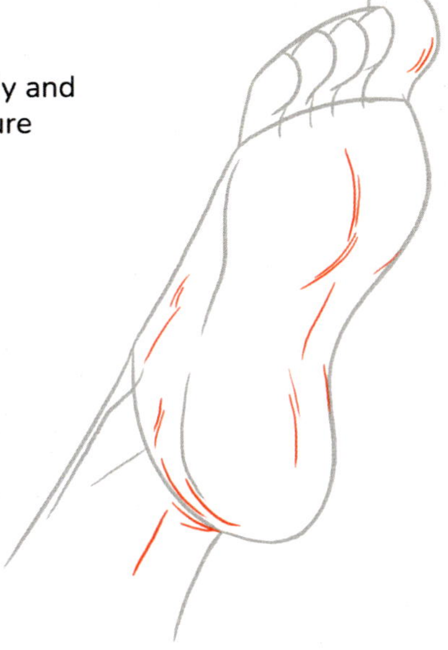

6.
Finalize the drawing!

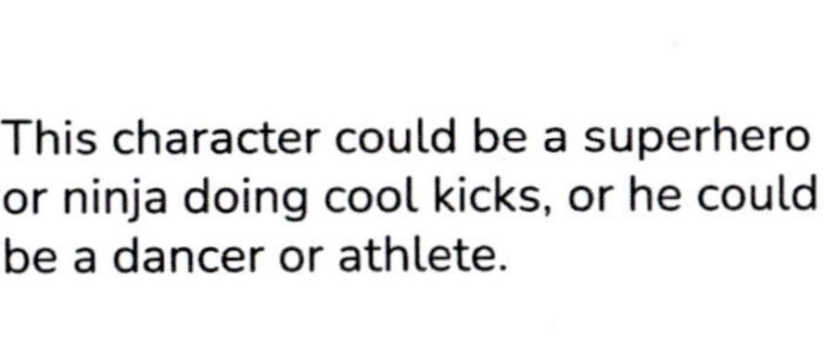

This character could be a superhero or ninja doing cool kicks, or he could be a dancer or athlete.

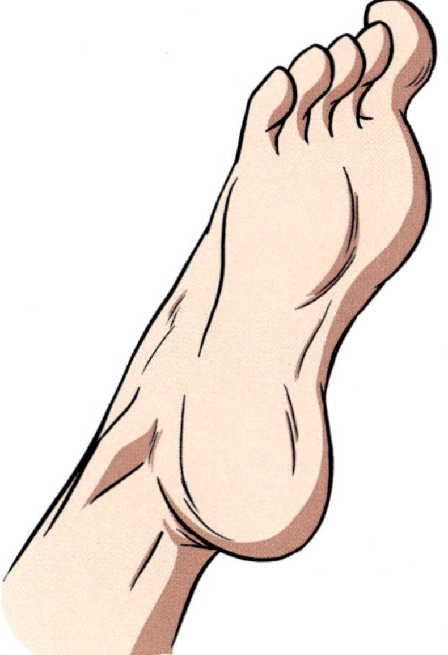

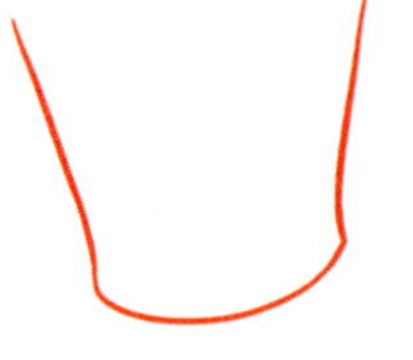

1.
Draw the lower leg tapering into the ankle. If you want your character to look strong, make the ankle thick.

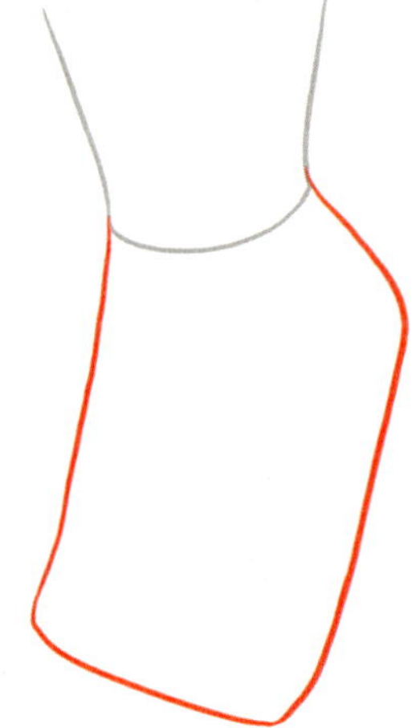

2.
Draw the foot as a round rectangle with a big curve for the heel.

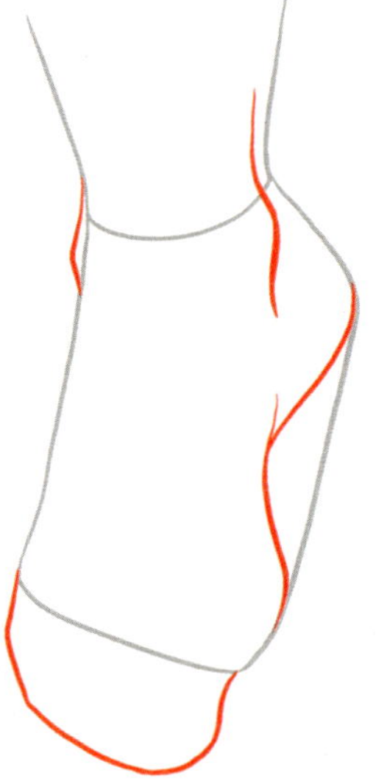

3.
Draw curves to show the foot's arch, then add the rectangular toe area.

Make bumps on both sides for the ankle bones.

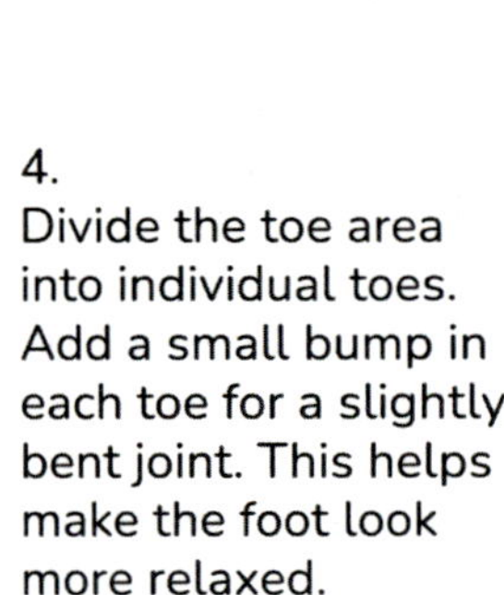

4.
Divide the toe area into individual toes. Add a small bump in each toe for a slightly bent joint. This helps make the foot look more relaxed.

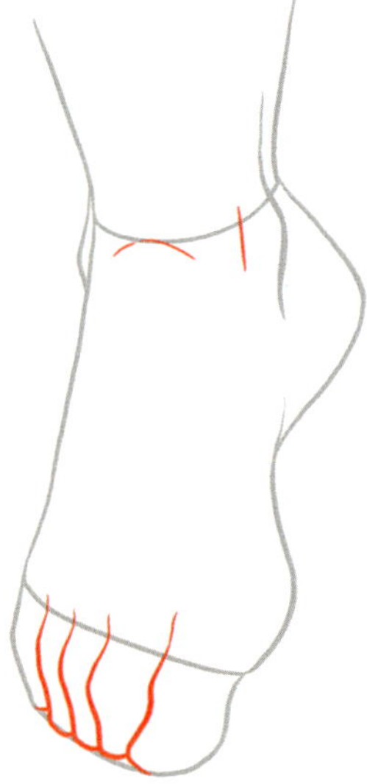

Foot Lifted + Relaxed

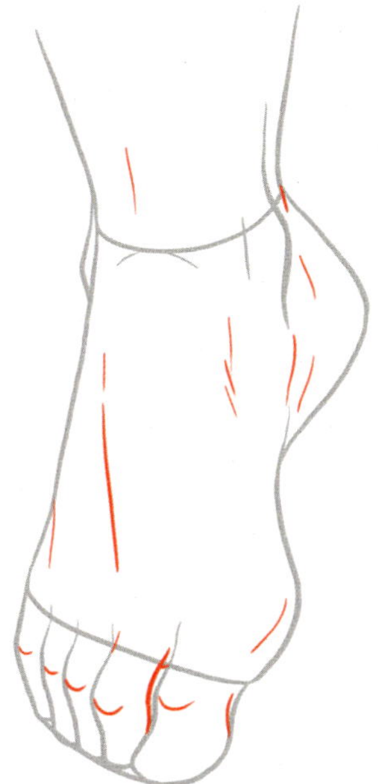

5.
Add texture and details to show joints and the foot's structure.

This is a great way to make your drawing look more realistic.

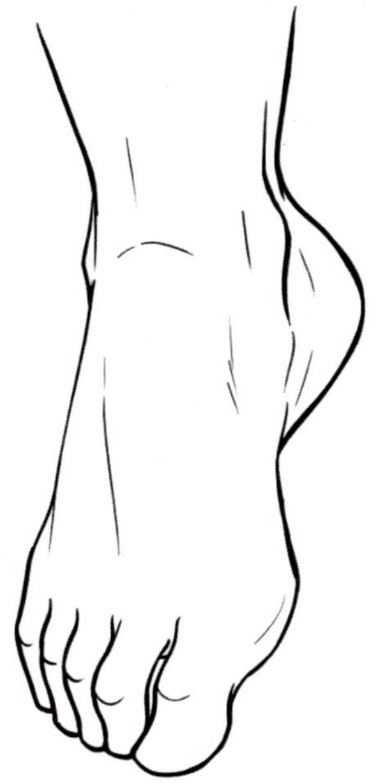

6.
After erasing extra lines, use a dark pen to go over the final drawing.

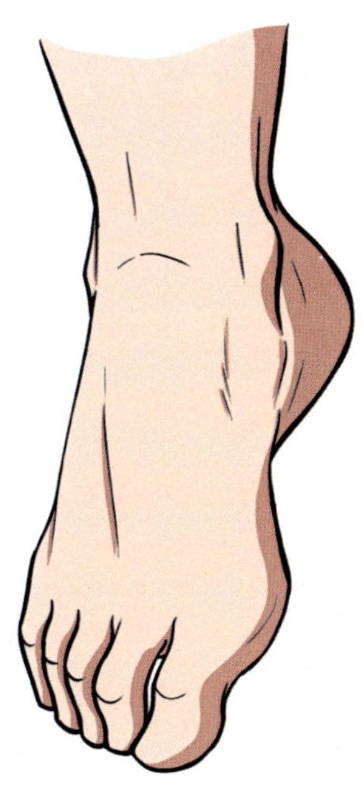

This pose can be for when a character is relaxed. He could be an angel or super-hero, hovering in the air, or he could be dipping his toe into a pool.

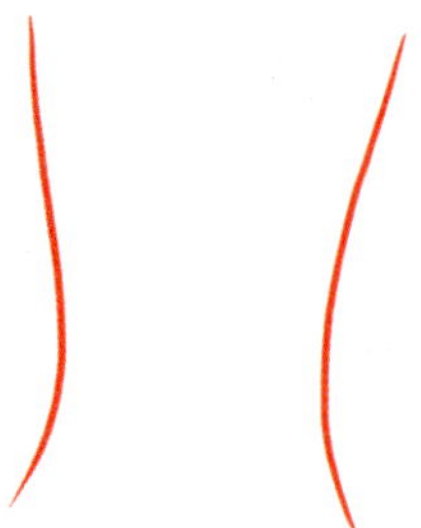

1.
Draw the ankle area tapered in the middle.

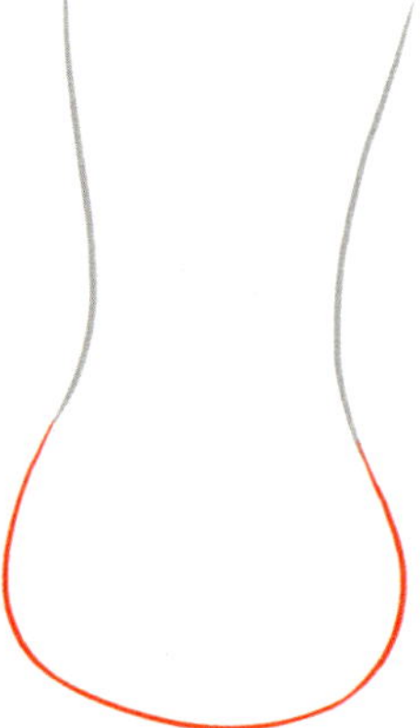

2.
Add a large round curve at the end. This is for the big heel.

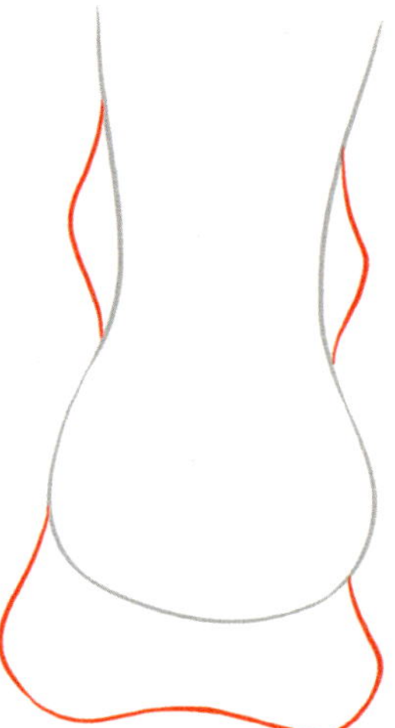

3.
Add the other part of the foot as a bumpy shape under the round heel. Then, draw ankle bones on both sides.

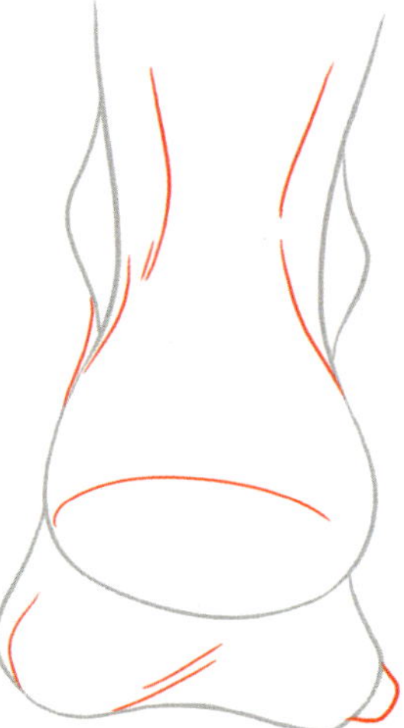

4.
Draw a small toe poking out at the side. Most of the toes will not show, but it's a good idea to draw a little bit of a toe for more dimension and realism. Draw more lines in the ankle and heel area.

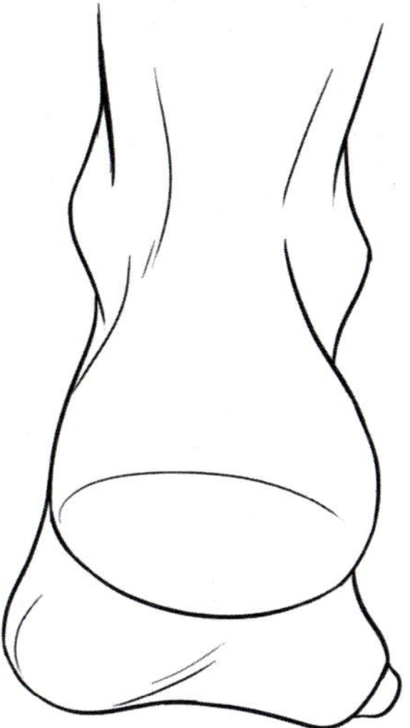

5.
Use a dark pen or marker to go over the final drawing.

This character could be walking, running, or tiptoeing, and the viewer is behind them.

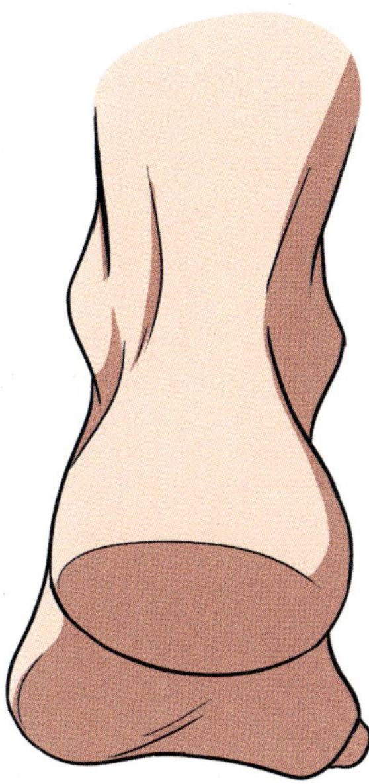

Back View Foot

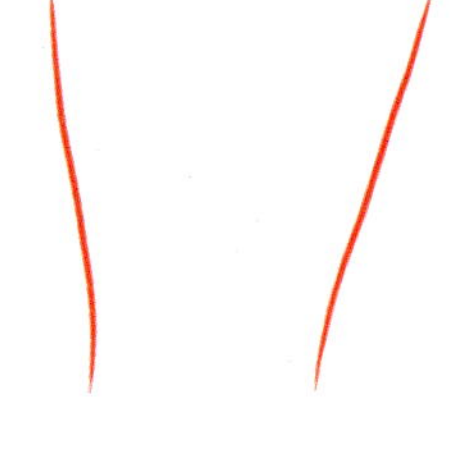

1.
Begin with the ankle area.

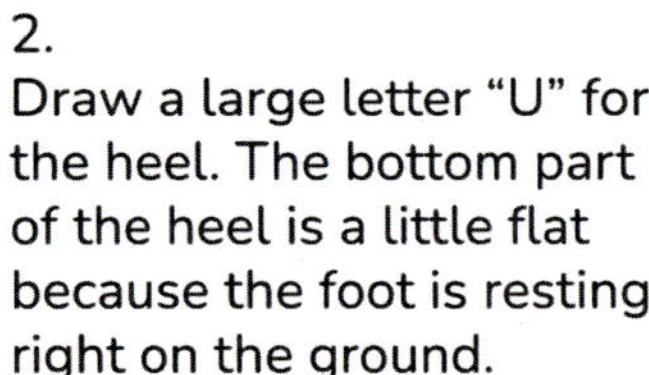

2.
Draw a large letter "U" for the heel. The bottom part of the heel is a little flat because the foot is resting right on the ground.

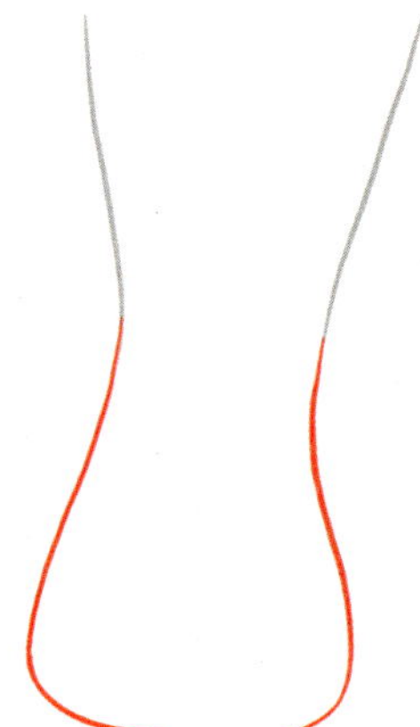

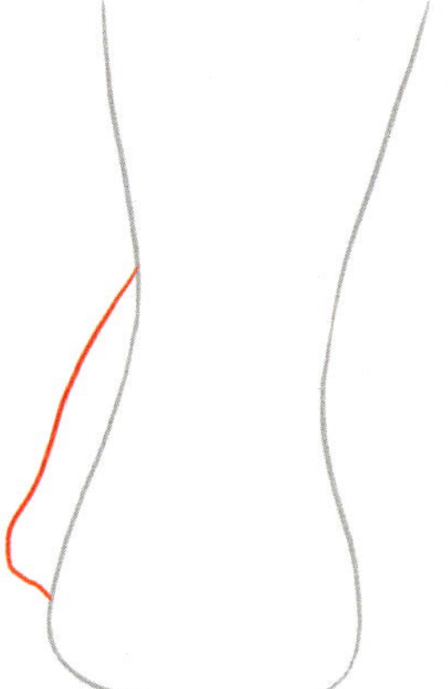

3.
Draw a little bit of the side of the foot.

It's a good idea to show this part, even in a back view, because this adds more dimension to your drawing.

4.
Now draw a small bit of the toe poking out from the front.

Then, draw ankle bones and lines to show the structure of the heel and joint area.

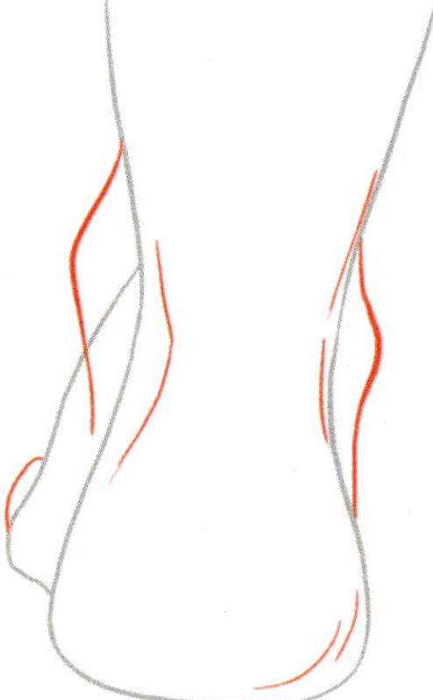

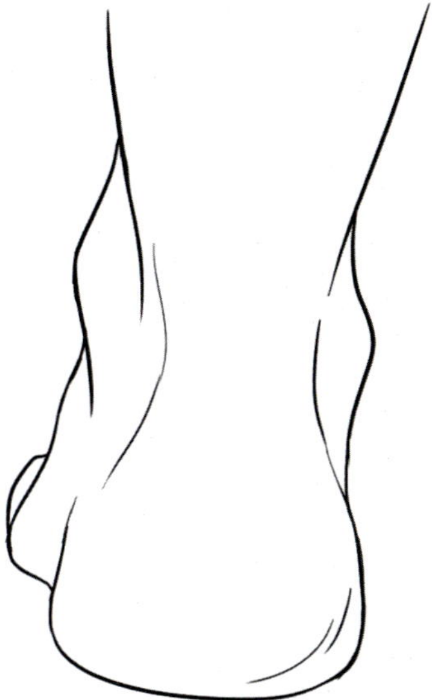

5.
Use a dark pen or marker to ink your drawing.

Usually, a back view can include parts of the side and front of the foot. This is a good way to show dimension and perspective.

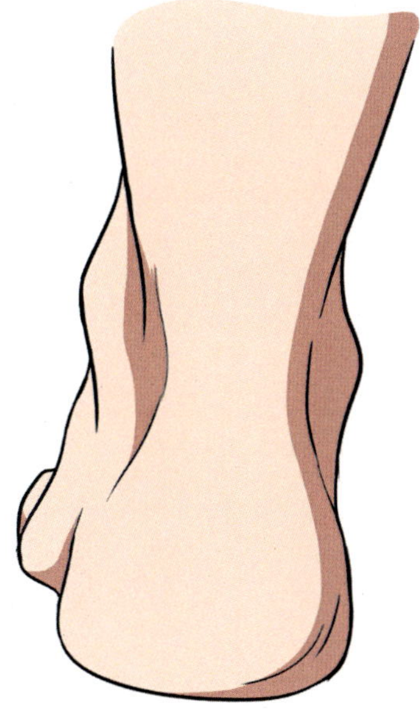

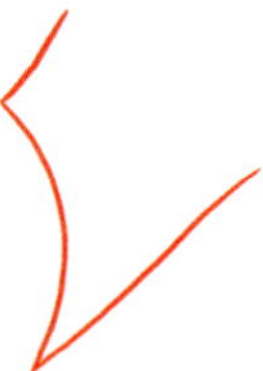

1.
Begin with the ankle tilted. Draw the lines coming in towards each other.

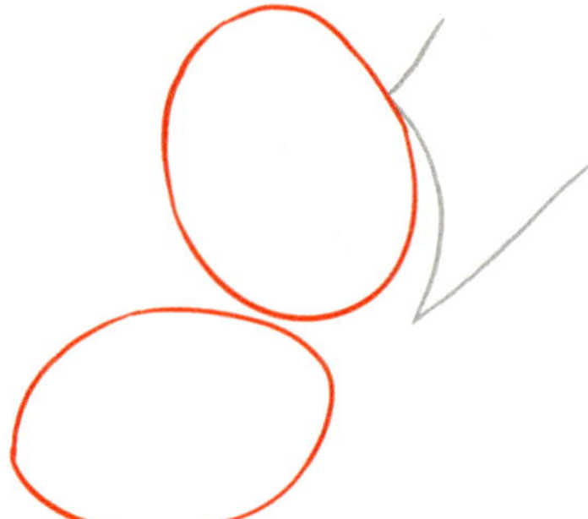

2.
Draw two large ovals for the foot to start. Angle them towards each other for a more natural pose.

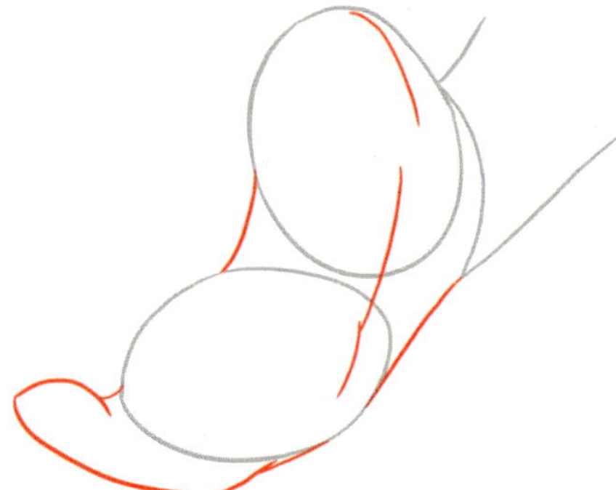

3.
Add lines to connect the two ovals together. Then, draw the curled toe area.

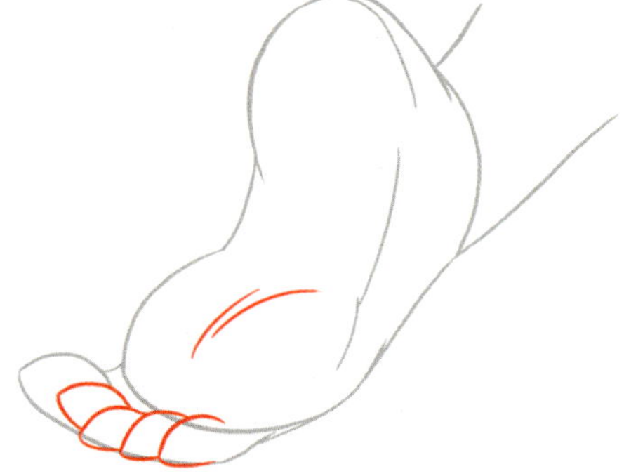

4.
Repeat curves for the toes. Make them go in slightly different angles so your foot looks more natural, and not too stiff.

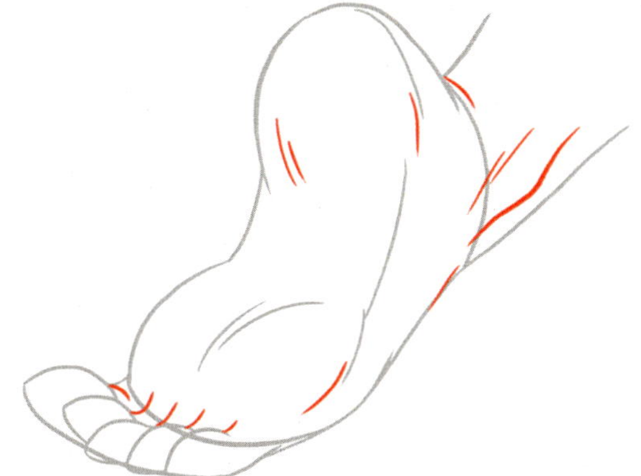

5.
Add more details and lines to show the texture and structure better for the foot and ankle. This also gives your drawing a more realistic look.

6.
When you're ready, use a dark pen to finalize your drawing.

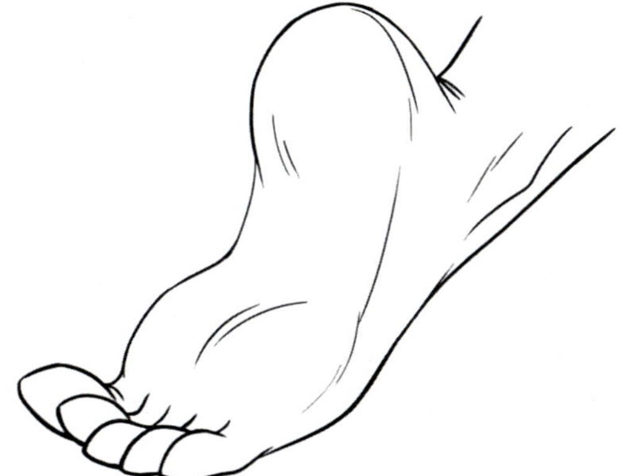

This character could be lying on the beach, on a bed, or the carpet.

He could also be leaping or diving forward quickly in an intense baseball game, or in a swimming competition.

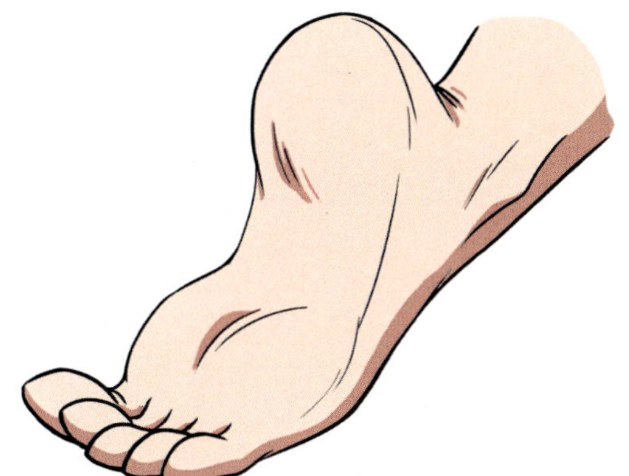

Tense Toes

BY MEI YU

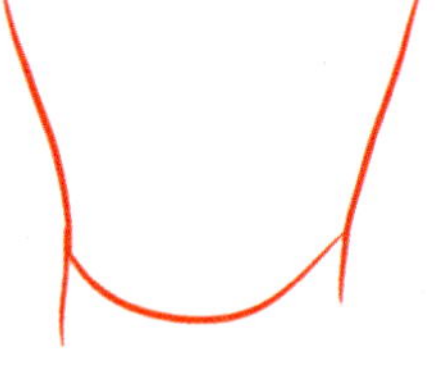

1.
Begin with the ankle. In this perspective, the lower leg lines will angle into the ankle more.

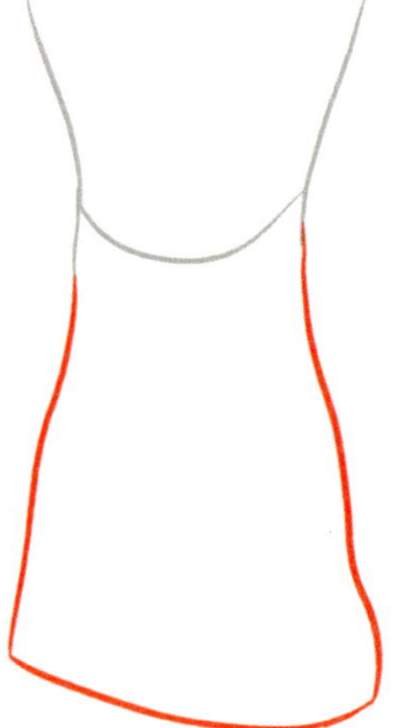

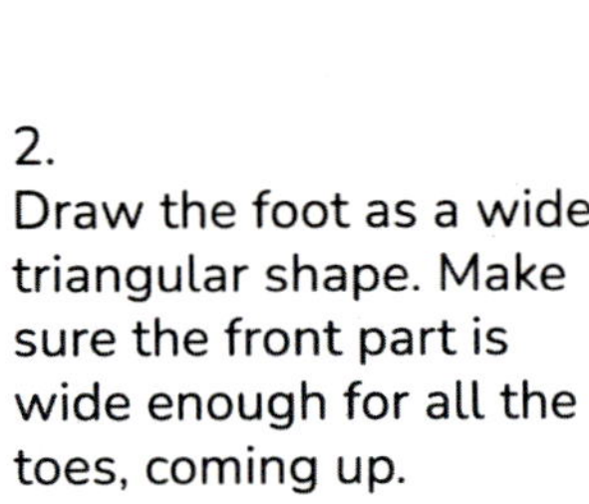

2.
Draw the foot as a wide triangular shape. Make sure the front part is wide enough for all the toes, coming up.

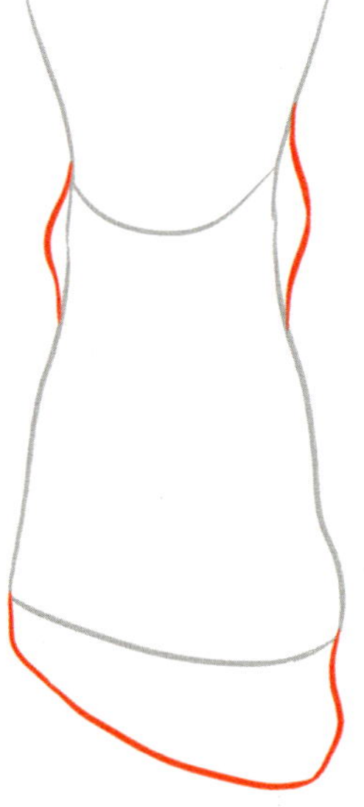

3.
Add the toe area like a wedge shape, then draw the ankle bones.

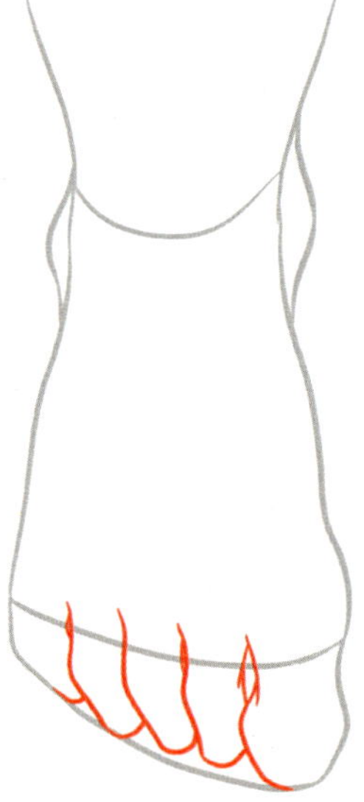

4.
Divide the toe area into the bent toes.

We'll add lines later to show the tension in the toes.

Tense Toes

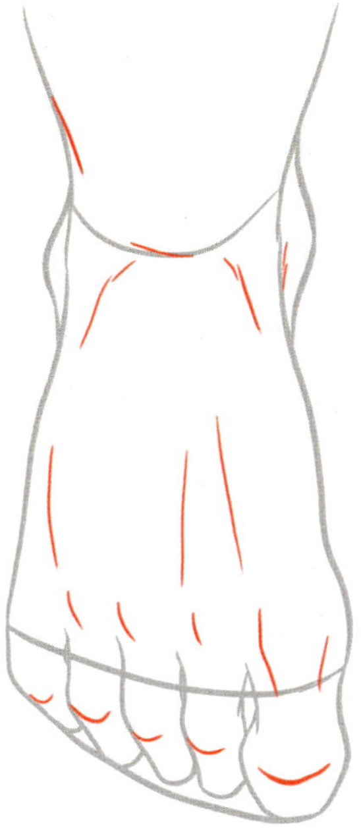

5.
Draw lines for the rigid tendons and joints in the toes and on top of the foot.

The more lines you add, the more tense the pose looks.

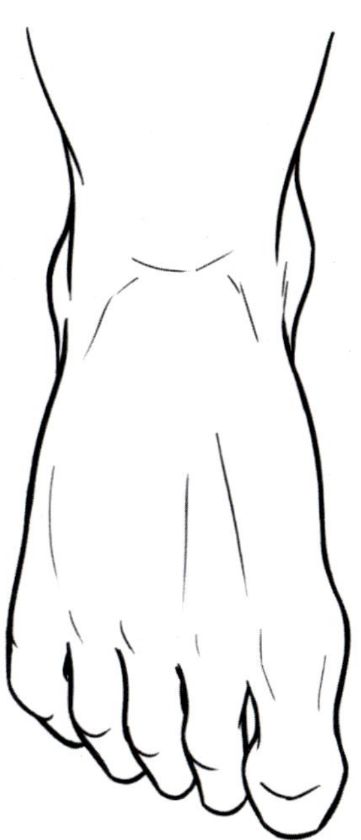

6.
When you're ready, ink the final drawing.

This pose shows how nervous or intense the character could be.

He could be standing on a tall diving board, his toes clutching the edge. Or, this character could be kicking up dirt in a battle or race.

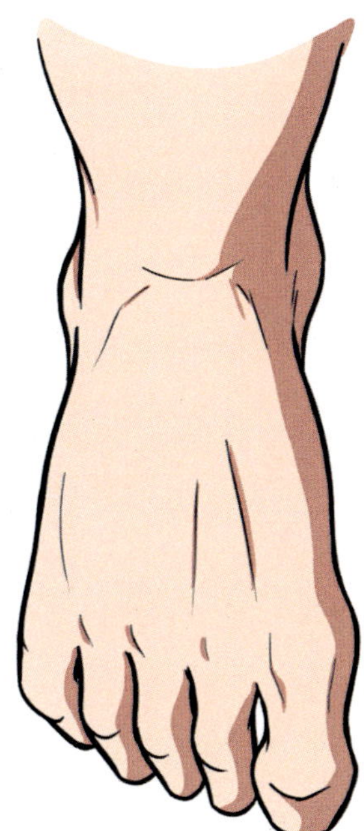

Foot Lifted (Back 3/4 View)

BY MEI YU

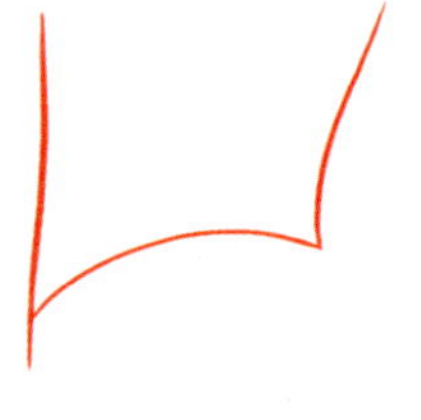

1.
Begin with the ankle tilted down.

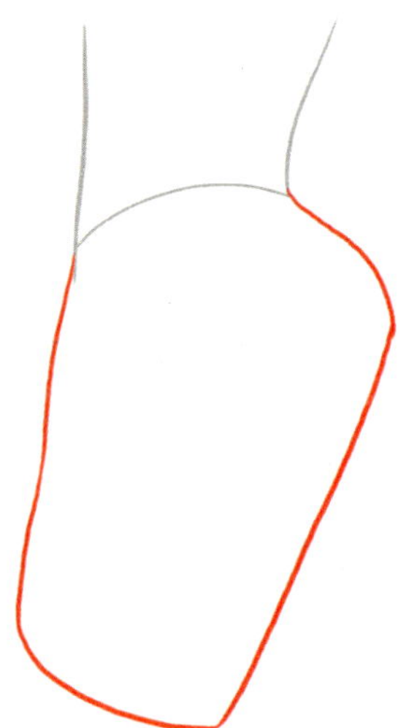

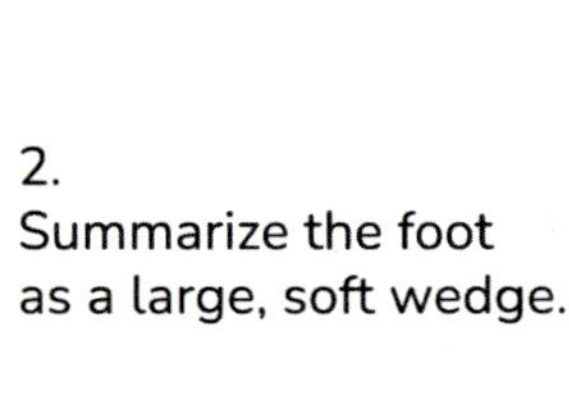

2.
Summarize the foot as a large, soft wedge.

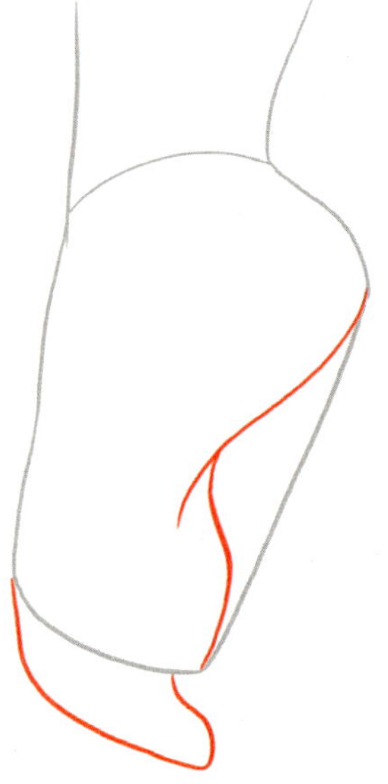

3.
Draw a big arch with two curves going into the wedge shape.

At the bottom, add the wide toe area.

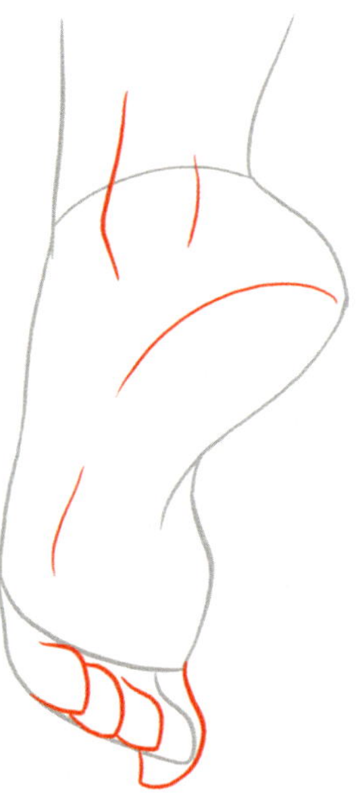

4.
Draw curves for all the smaller toes, then add a big toe pointing down.

Add more lines in the foot to show the edges and structure.

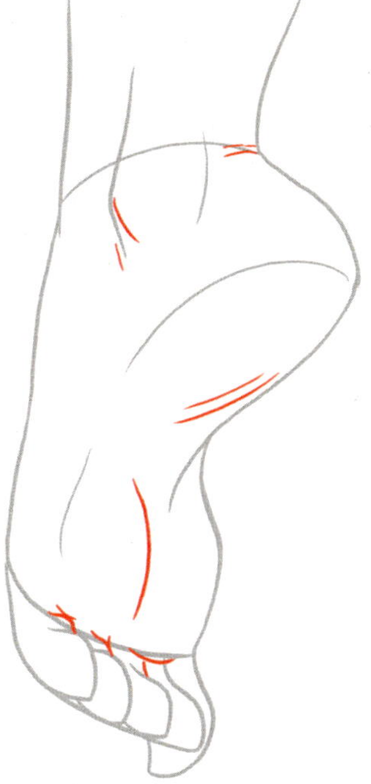

5.
Add finishing details for more realism.

Draw curves to show how the parts of the foot bend and fold.

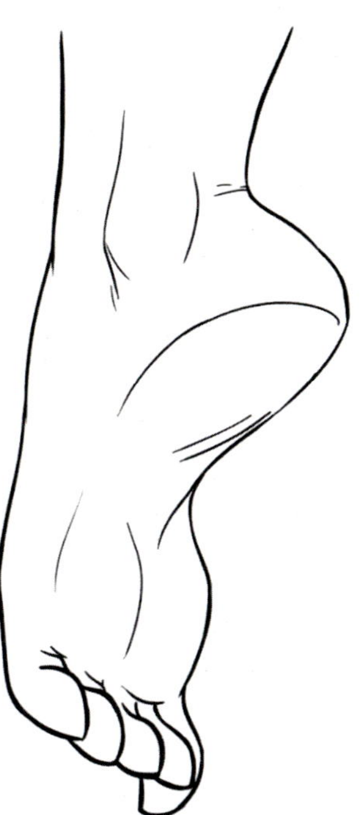

6.
Ink your awesome foot drawing!

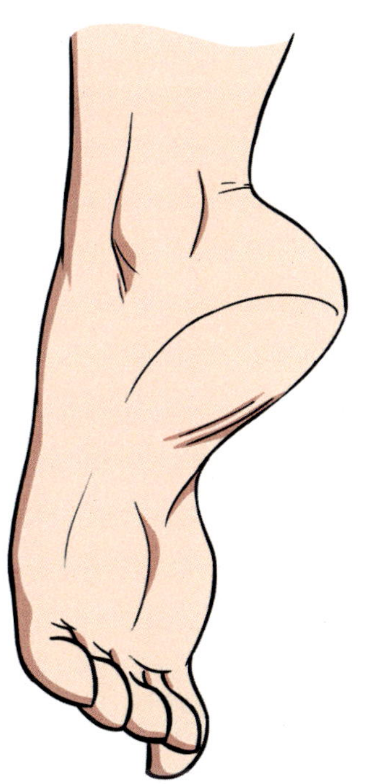

This is a nice view of a lifted foot. The character could be dipping his toe in water, or flying in the air.

Tilt it horizontally, and he could be lying and relaxing on a couch.

BY MEI YU

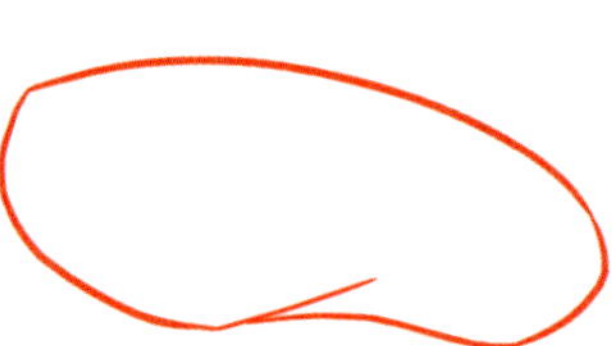

1.
Begin the first part of the foot with a squashed, lopsided bean shape.

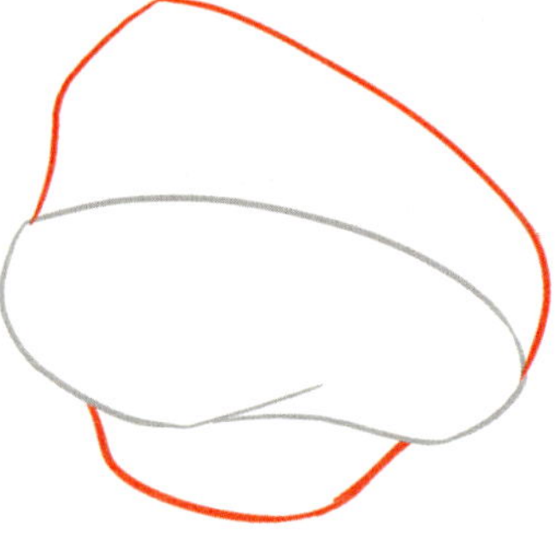

2.
Add a large, pointy toe shape, then draw the heel in the distance as a small bump.

Making the heel small in this pose is a great way to show the forced perspective.

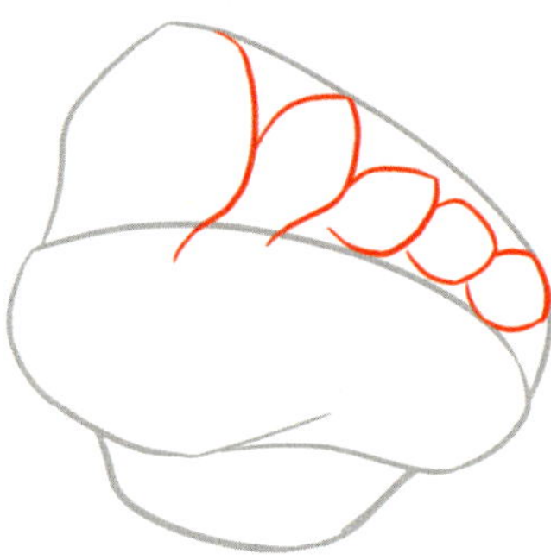

3.
In the large toe area, divide the individual toes. The big toe is curved and wide. Make the other toes get smaller as you go down.

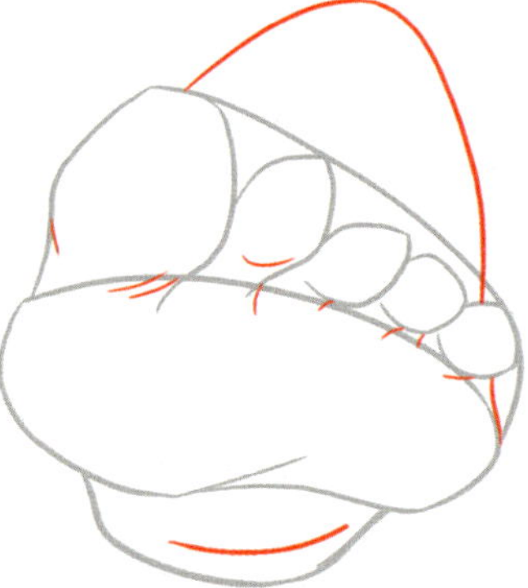

4.
Draw a large, pointy triangle above the toes. This is the top part of the foot. It will attach to the ankle area, coming up.

Then, add small lines for texture in the foot.

5.
Draw curved lines to indicate the ankle joint area.

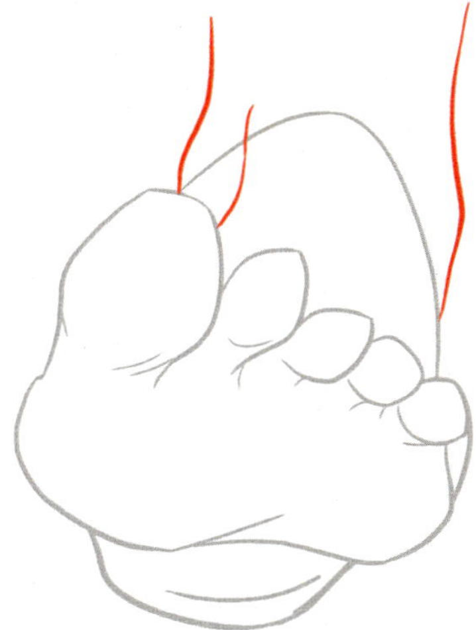

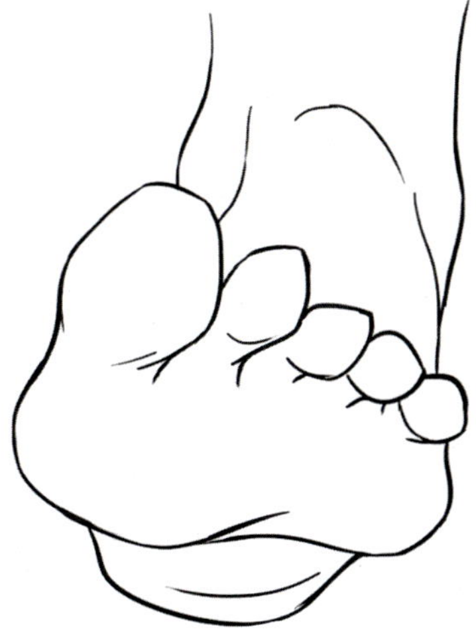

6.
Use a dark pen to ink your drawing. Try making the small texture lines thin for a realistic feel.

This is a cool pose to try if your character is kicking something right at the viewer.

It's engaging and dynamic!

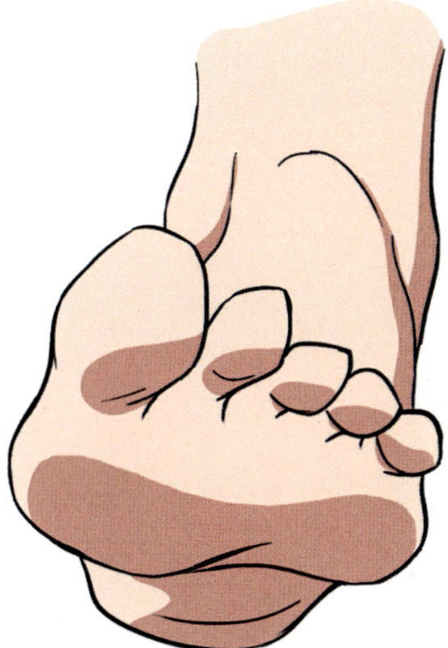

Paperbacks

Mei Yu's Book Store

Over 80 books!

Coloring Books

New Releases

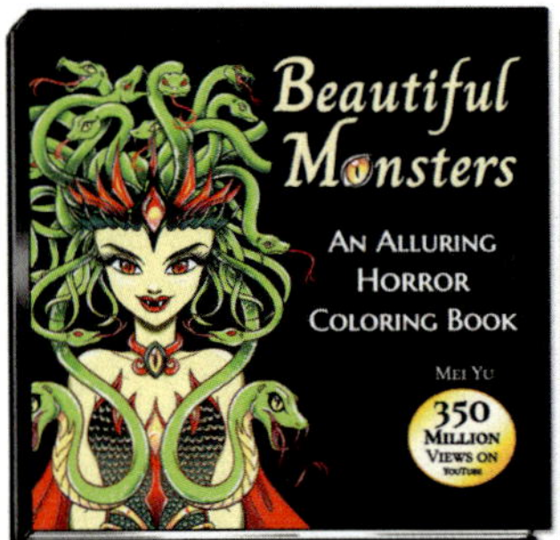

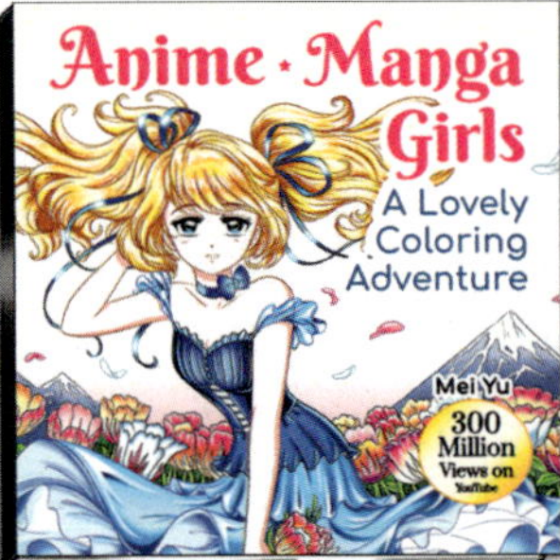

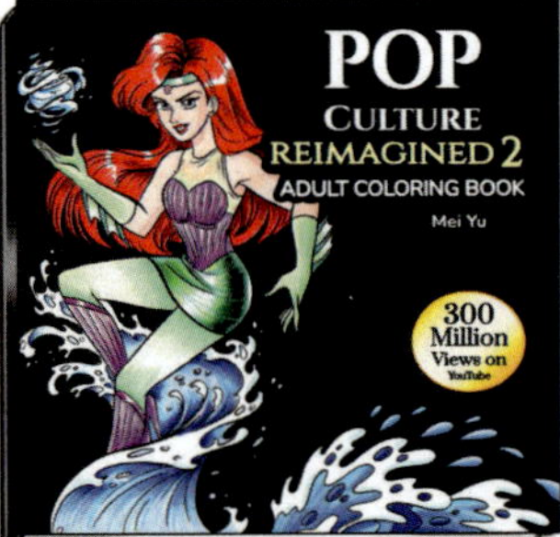

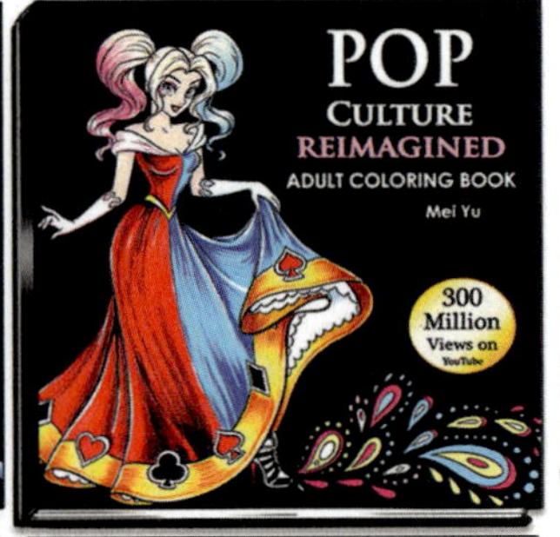

©Mei Yu Art Inc.

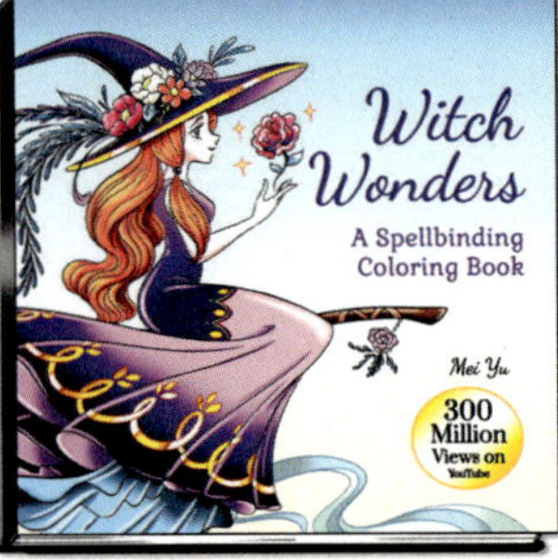

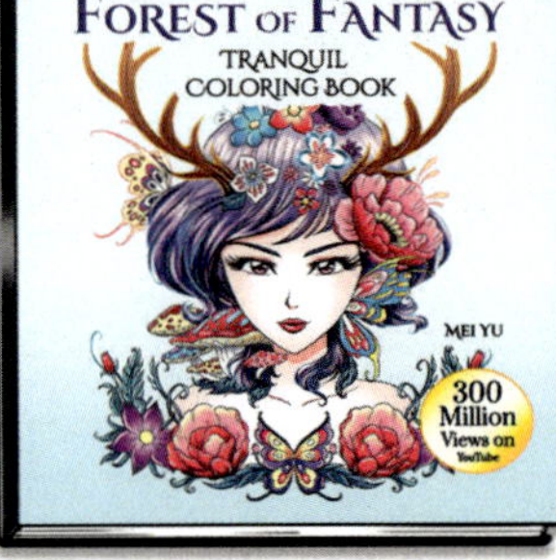

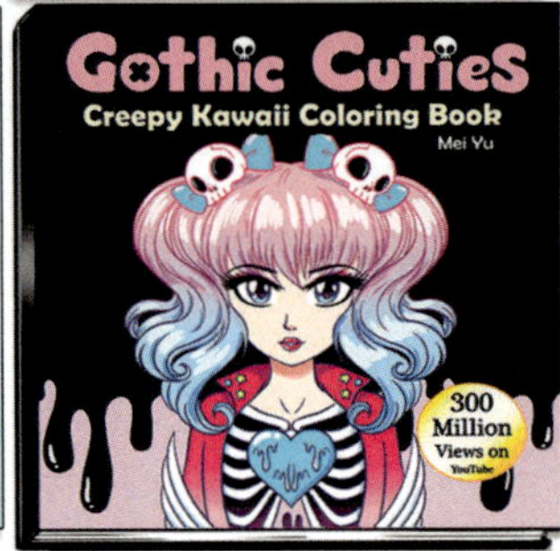

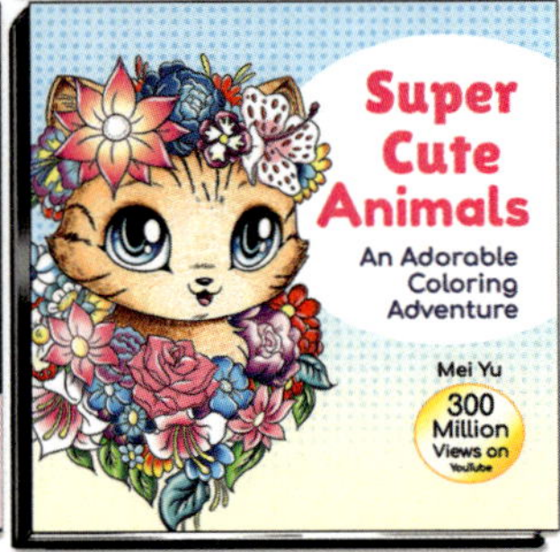

AND MORE...

Other sizes + hardcovers also available

How to Draw Books

New Release

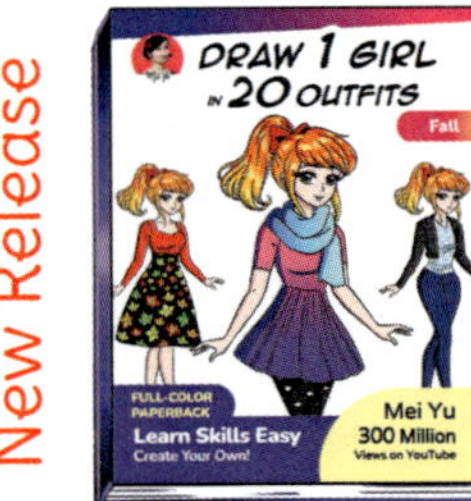

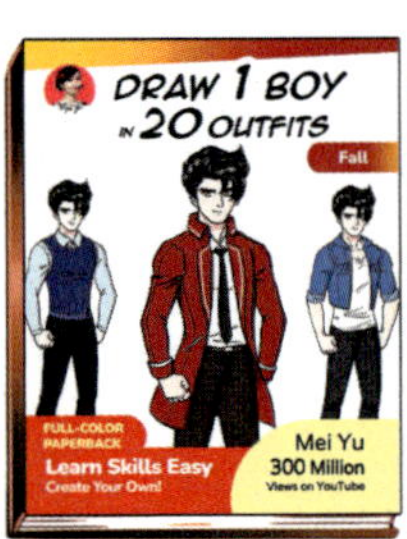

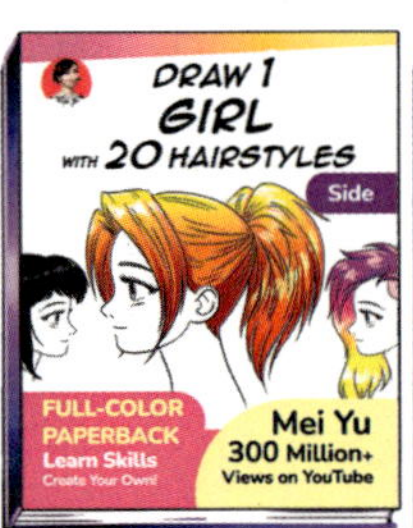

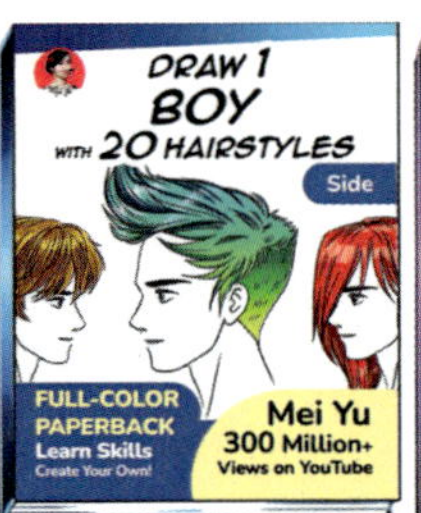

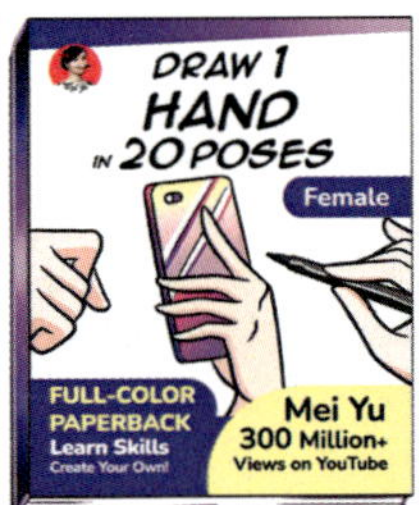

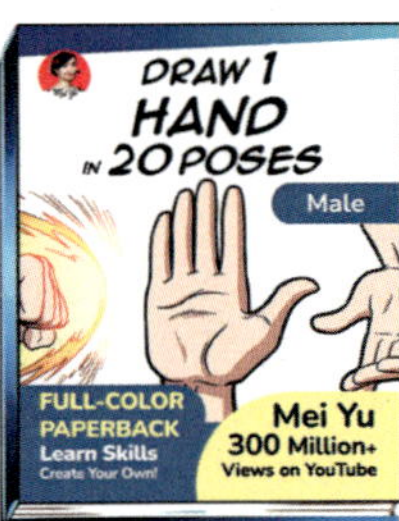

WorkBooks

New Release

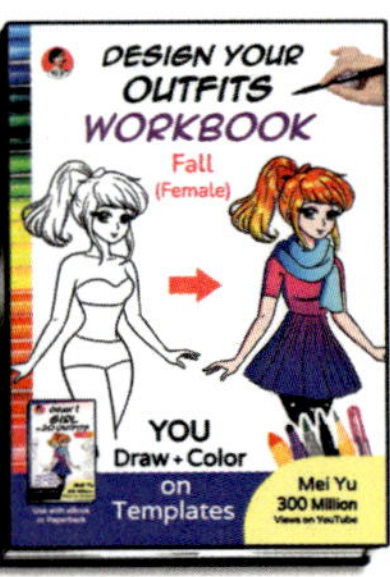

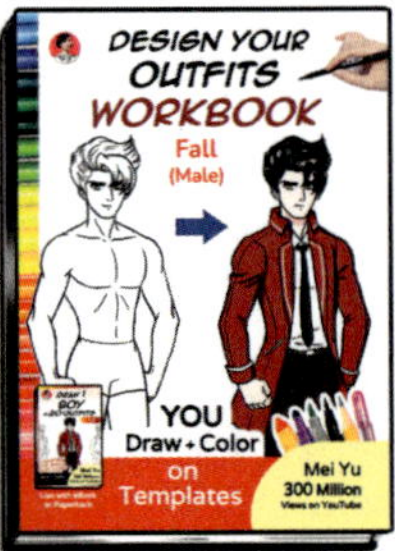

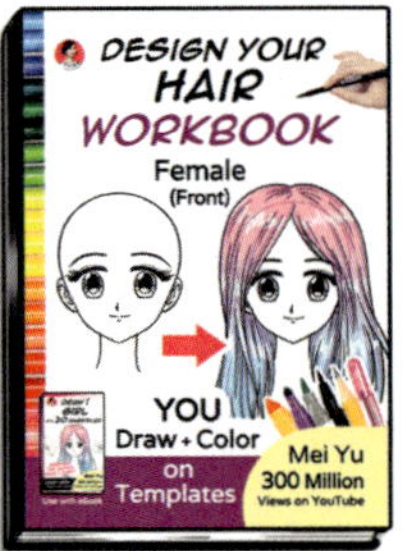

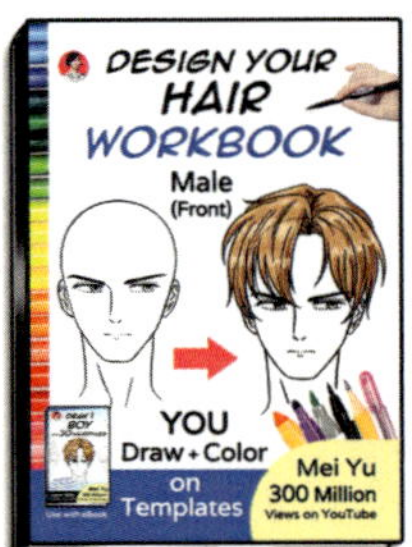

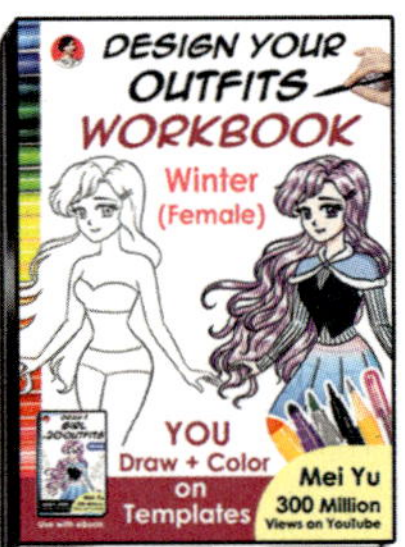

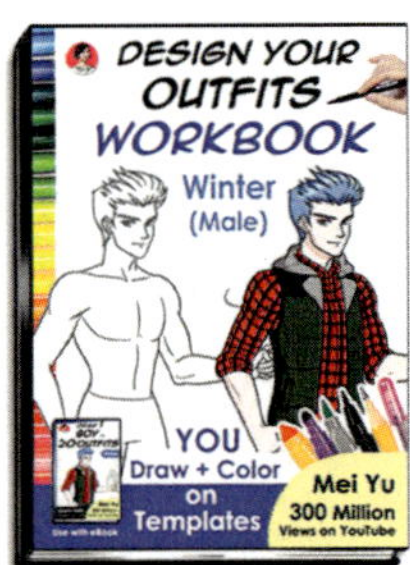

AND MORE...

Unleash Your Creativity  Own Now or Gift!

available at
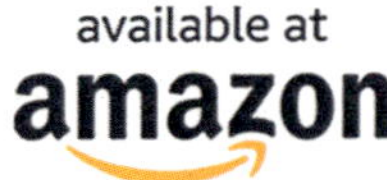

www.amazon.com/shop/meiyu

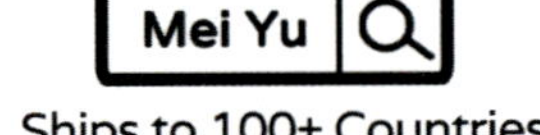

Ships to 100+ Countries

★ DRAW 1 IN 20 SERIES

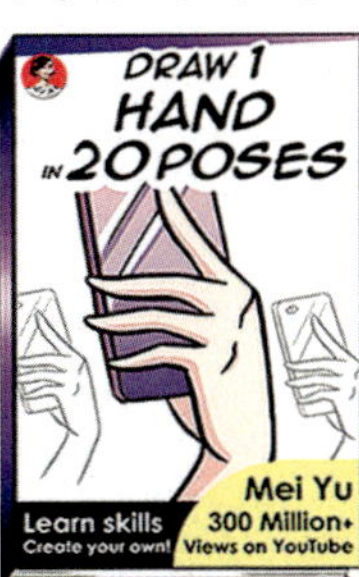

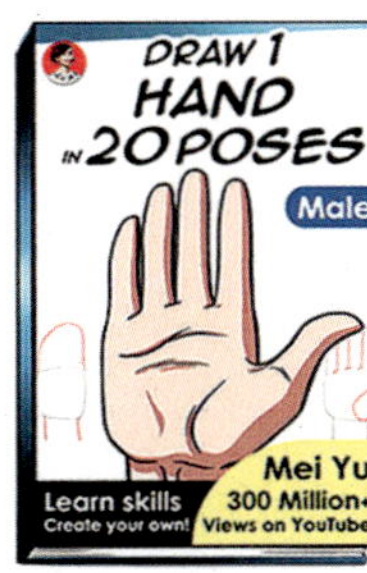

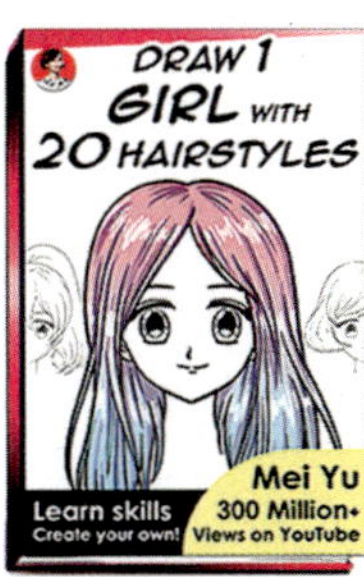

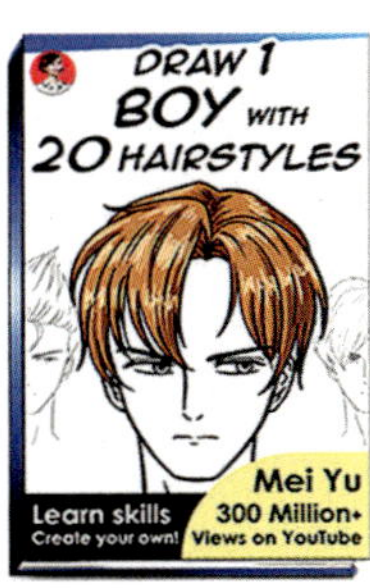

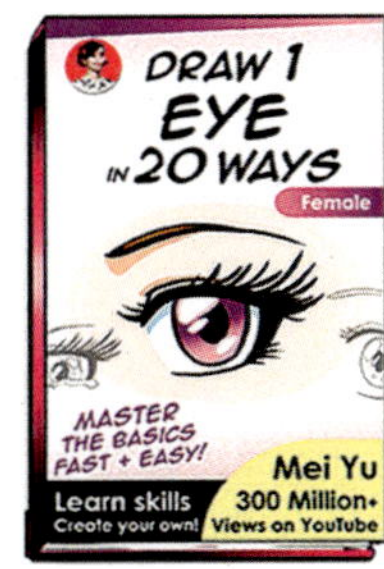

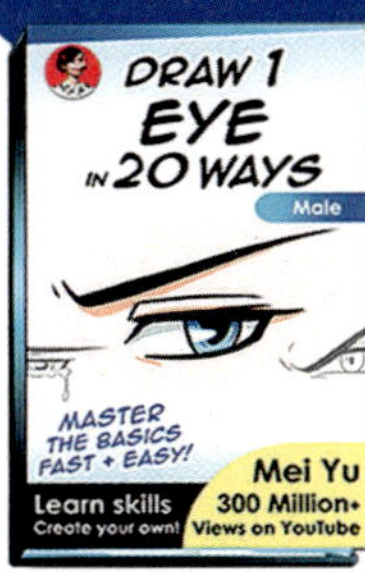

AND MORE...

★ Draw Reimagined Characters Series

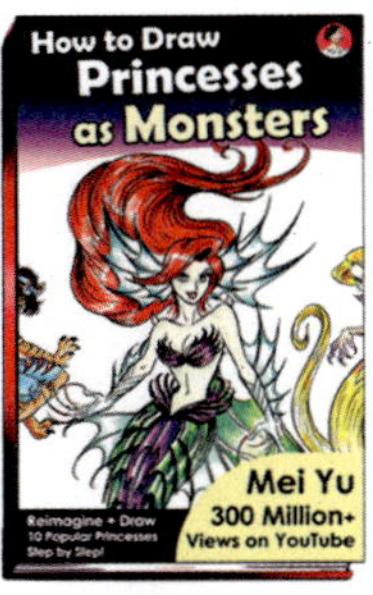

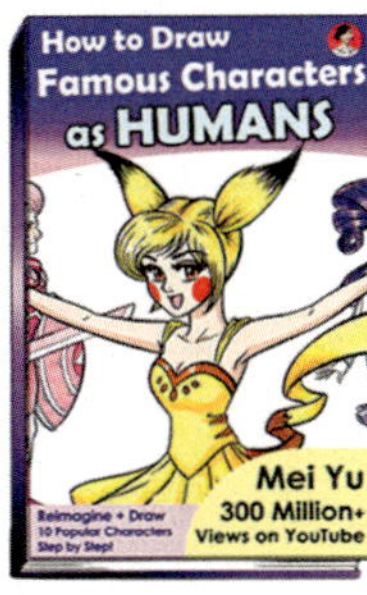

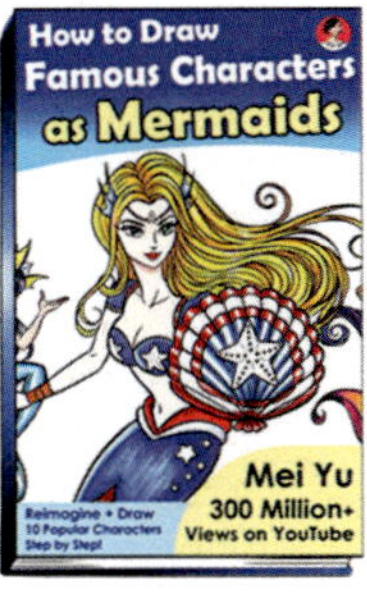

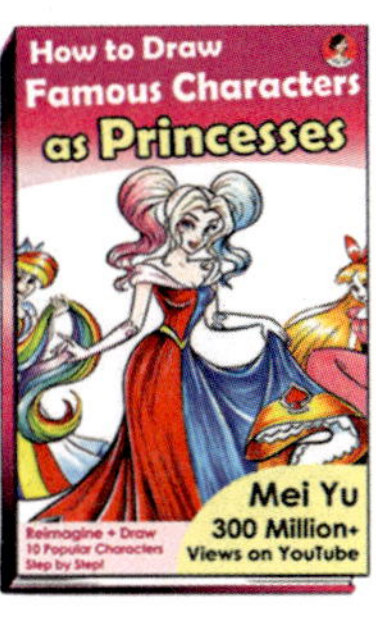

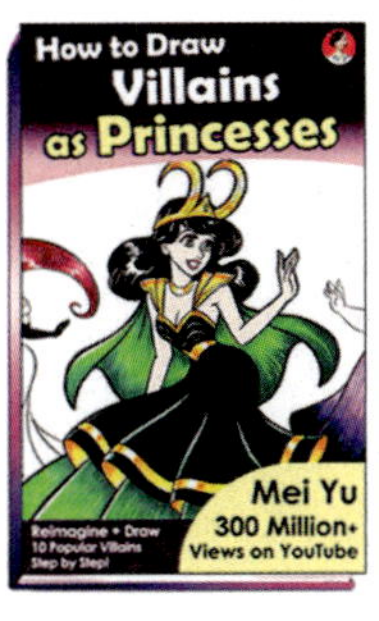

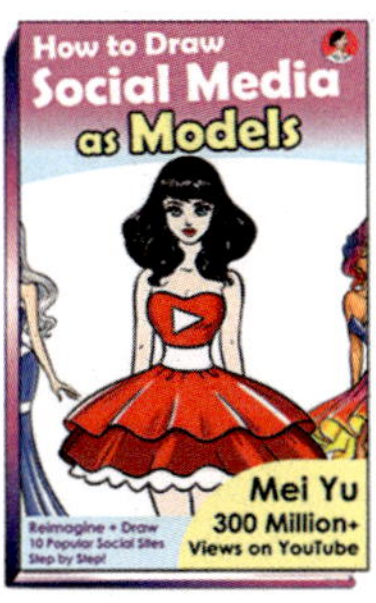

AND MORE...

★ 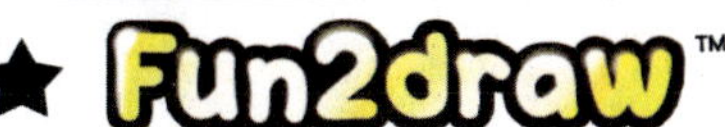 Series

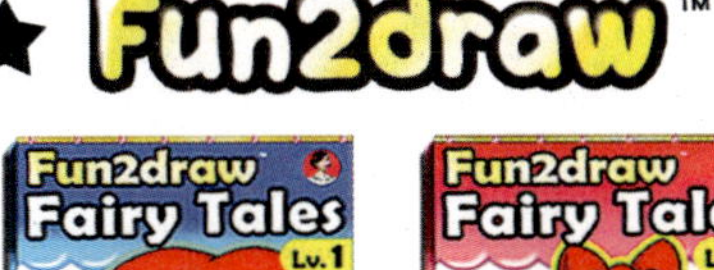

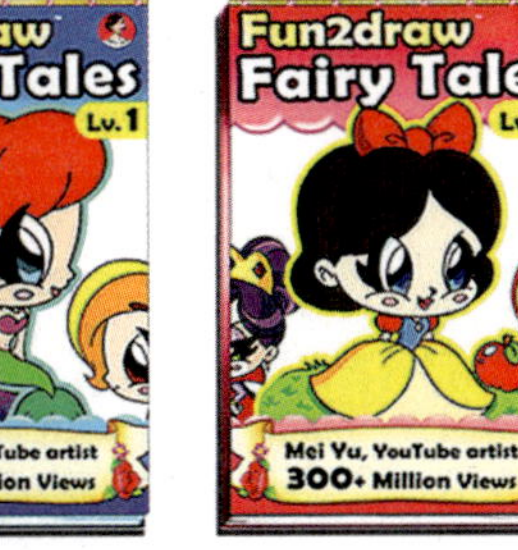

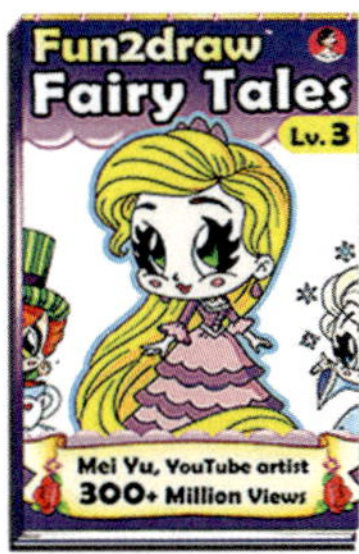

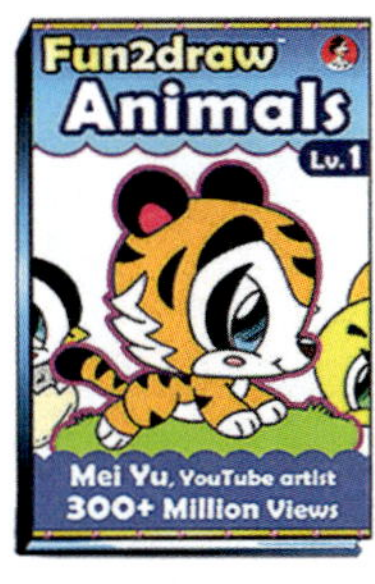

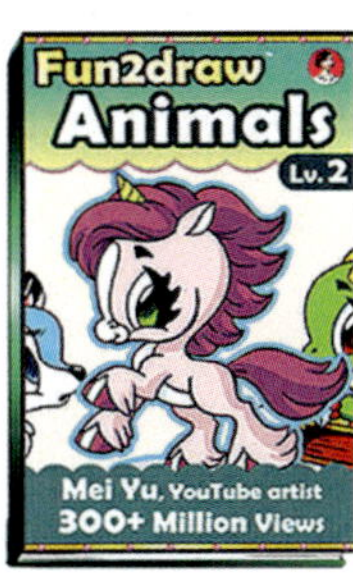

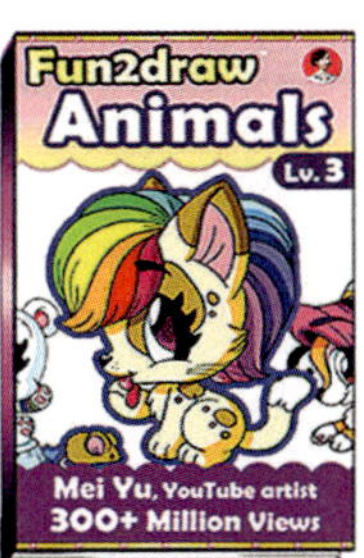

AND MORE...

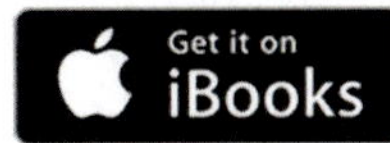

https://itunes.apple.com/us/author/mei-yu/id1055789735

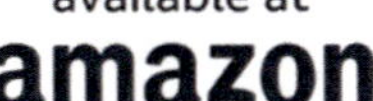

https://www.amazon.com/shop/meiyu

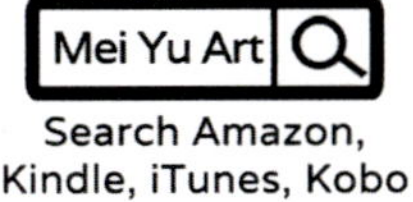

Search Amazon, Kindle, iTunes, Kobo

Android™ users: Download the Kindle App to get my eBooks

Kobo users: Search "Mei Yu Art" in the Kobo app or Kobo website

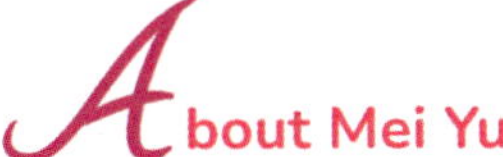

About Mei Yu

Mei Yu started drawing on walls at age 2. She is a diverse artist and designer from Canada. Mei also has a popular YouTube art channel **www.youtube.com/MeiYu** with over 1.5 million subscribers, 800 videos, and 350 million views.

Mei is happy to know that many fans are inspired by her art and books, and that they are encouraged to pursue art.

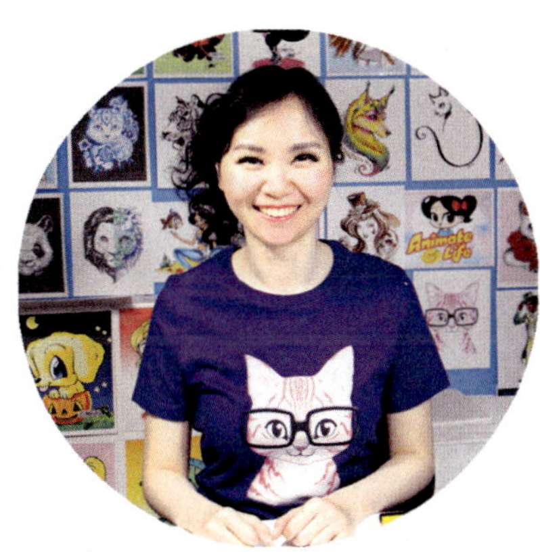

Made in the USA
Monee, IL
20 November 2022